Foundations of
REVIVAL

6TH EDITION

Biblical Evidence of Revival

Jeanne Metcalf

1st Edition 2014

6th Edition (updated)
International Copyright © 2024
Cegullah Publishing & Apologetics Academy
All rights reserved.

ISBN # Textbook: 978-1-926489-52-0
ISBN # Workbook: 978-1-926489-53-7

COPYRIGHT MATTERS

This book is an original manuscript by the author, protected by international copyright laws of Canada. Therefore, none of this author's work may be reproduced, in part or in whole, or stored in a retrieval system, or transmitted in any form or by any means, electronic, mechanical, photocopied, recorded or otherwise for commercial use without the *prior written* permission of the author. However, it is possible to receive permission to use short quotations for personal use, or use in a study group study, or for permission to copy certain passages, or to make portions of the writings available for overhead viewing. Simply, contact the author[1] to request it.

Note: While the charts might not be marked nevertheless, they are copyrighted, too.

SCRIPTURE MATTERS

All scripture quotes *originate* from KJV, public domain. However, the name of God appears as YeHoVaH, not LORD. See appendix for more information.

---

[1] See Contact Page in Appendix

ABOUT THIS BOOK

This book, now an accredited course available at Cegullah Publishing & Apologetic Academy, serves as a textbook for Course 105, as well as for all students who wish to study the topic of Revival, unaccredited.

For those studying unaccredited, it is better to obtain the workbook, too. This gives the serious student a deeper understanding of the topic and helps the student to come away with a greater understanding of the topic of Revival.

Please note: All instructions for Degree Students are found, as usual, within the Workbook.

For more information contact
Cegullah Publishing @ cegullapublsihing.ca

DEDICATION

This book is dedicated, first to the Living God, Yeshua Ha' Mashiach, Who is worthy of a people to follow Him with all their heart, mind, soul, and strength; and secondly to every serious Christian believer wishing to attain their full destiny in God, living and walking in the power of the Holy Spirit, turning the world upside down as they spread the gospel message of salvation to every nation.

COURSE # 105
FOUNDATIONS OF REVIVAL
TABLE OF CONTENTS

TITLE	PAGE
Introduction...	9
Special Note...	12
SECTION 1	
1. Revival's Call	15
2. Revival's Promise...................................	43
SECTION 2	
3. Identifying Revival...............................	
Marking Revival's Beginnings.....	83
Pre-Revival Traits...........................	99
Early Revival Traits........................	111
Full-Fledged Revival Traits...........	117
SECTION 3	
4. New Covenant Revival..........................	133
5. Revival and "You".................................	169

APPENDIX

About King James Version……………	201
About the Author……………………...	214
A Name to Honour……………………	195
Chart Reference Guide..…………….…	210
Contact Information…………………..	215
Index of Hebrew Words ……………...	211
Other Books by This Author………….	211
Salvation's Message……………….…...	202
Scriptures Index…………….................	208
Sinner's Prayer & Commitment……...	206

INTRODUCTION

Many Christian believers today long for Revival, in that they expect to see the power of God released in many powerful ways including a supernatural ability to harvest lost souls. To those, longing for this Revival, it is but a breath away! On the opposite spectrum, there are believers who think Revival will never come. These believe the Apostolic writers never spoke about Revival, and thus, we should not expect to see it today. Which of these two groups is correct?

To answer that question, we will <u>not</u> approach the subject by looking at past Revivals of the last few centuries. While the evidence of historical Revivals, in our not-too-distant past, intrigues us as it speaks of mighty signs and wonders, these cannot be our pattern for Revival. Since the canon of scripture closed, those Revivals, no matter how accurately recorded, are not exonerated like scripture and thus, these fall into the category of hearsay evidence.

All manifestations, goals, insights and events of any Revival must coordinate with the whole counsel of God found within the Word of God, and thus, with that counsel in mind, we safely enjoy and experience it. Only within the parameters of the Word of God then, do we know God's point of view on Revival.

This details how Revival begins and functions, and it includes the desired response of us, His children. Knowing what God says first, within the bible background, we have our pattern or blueprint, and the application for our generation.

This book, "Foundations of Revival", investigates Revival from a biblical perspective, studying many scriptural passages, Hebraic and Apostolic[2], which describes Revival, *from God's point of view*.

It then, applies it to the Body of Messiah[3], making it practical for believers today. The many scriptural passages, about Revival, are too numerous to examine one by one, but the ones studied here give enough scripture to define a biblical blueprint for Revival. When finished, the reader should know how to read the signs of Revival to identify it, know the true

---

[2] First Covenant, Second or Renewed or New Covenant, depending on your terminology.

[3] To understand this term, please read the special note in this chapter.

purpose of it, understand how it operated in the past bible days under *both Covenants,* and how *God intends it* to operate today.

The rewards, for the time spent studying Revival, manifests in a broadened understanding of "God's perspective" of Revival. Readers, approaching the subject of Revival to experience it, do so with a confidence of the biblical manifestations of Revival, as a whole, and on a personal level. Their knowledge of this important subject then, rests upon a good foundation, on which to perceive and understand, and experience Revival.

SPECIAL NOTE
There are some words, used in this book, whose meaning must be clarified:

THE "BODY OF MESSIAH"
- This term also refers to believers, those embers of the body of Messiah (Christ)

THE WORD "CHURCH":
- Refers to the overall body of believers in Messiah (Christ)
- Is **NOT** a reference to any individual church denomination or church building

THE WORD "EKKLESIA"
- This word means, "the called out ones"
- The called out ones are believers in Messiah
- The use of this word refers to the collective body of believers in the world

HEBRAIC SCRIPTURES:
- This term refers to the authors of the books from Genesis to Yeshua's arrival.

APOSTOLIC SCRIPTURES:
- This term refers to the authors of the books from Matthew to Revelation

NEW COVENANT:
- Jeremiah prophesied about a covenant. He used the word "חָדָשׁ" *(khaw-dash')*, meaning renewed, like the new moon in the heavens. Yeshua is the sacrifice of that renewed or new or covenant.

To understand the heart of this book, and the Intentions of the author, please keep these words and their *intended meaning* in mind.

SECTION 1

REVIVAL'S CALL   1

*Come, and let us **return** unto YeHoVaH: for he hath **torn**, and he will **heal** us; he hath **smitten**, and he will **bind** us up. After two days will he **revive us**: in the third day he will **raise** us up, and we shall **live** in his **sight**. Then shall we know, if we **follow on** to know YeHoVaH: his **going forth** is prepared as the morning; and he shall **come** unto us as the **rain**, as the latter and former rain unto the earth.*[4]

Hosea 6:1-3

In this passage, the promise of Revival began with a definite and clear invitation to God's people to come and to return to YeHoVaH, the covenant God of Israel. That invitation, or call, echoing from the lips of God's prophet, Hosea, reveals both the heart of God and outlines the need for a response from the people living

---

[4] Please note that PROMISED REVIVAL never came to Northern Israel in the time of Hosea.

in covenant with God. When heeded, that call to Revival, promised to establish the people of God on an amazing journey. The result of that promised divine healing, and more importantly, a fulfilling and prosperous relationship with God. All of that, however, depended upon the people's response to the invitation to come and to return to YeHoVaH.

To understand the need for Israel's return and their subsequent journey with God, we must understand why God, in the first place, extended an invitation to His People. To do that, we must examine the promise within this scripture in its original setting in the history of Israel. This, then, will give us an idea of some of the fundamentals of this First Covenant call and promise of revival.

BACKGROUND TO THE BOOK OF HOSEA

In the time of Hosea, and for a long time prior to Hosea's prophecies, Israel was a divided Nation. To understand the full impact of Hosea, and the context in which our scripture quote from Hosea 6:1-3 applies, we must look at the circumstances surrounding that division.

1 Kings 11:26-39	"26 ¶ And Jeroboam the son of Nebat, an Ephrathite of Zereda, Solomon's servant, whose mother's name *was*

Zeruah, a widow woman, even he lifted up *his* hand against the king. 27 And this *was* the cause that he lifted up *his* hand against the king: Solomon built Millo, *and* repaired the breaches of the city of David his father.

28 And the man Jeroboam *was* a mighty man of valour: and Solomon seeing the young man that he was industrious, he made him ruler over all the charge of the house of Joseph. 29 And it came to pass at that time when Jeroboam went out of Jerusalem, that the prophet Ahijah the Shilonite found him in the way; and he had clad himself with a new garment; and they two *were* alone in the field:

30 And Ahijah caught the new garment that *was* on him, and rent it *in* twelve pieces: 31 And he said to Jeroboam, Take thee ten pieces: for thus saith YeHoVaH, the God of Israel, Behold, I will rend the kingdom out of the hand of Solomon, and will give ten tribes to thee: 32 (But

he shall have one tribe for my servant David's sake, and for Jerusalem's sake, the city which I have chosen out of all the tribes of Israel:)

33 Because that they have forsaken me, and have worshipped Ashtoreth the goddess of the Zidonians, Chemosh the god of the Moabites, and Milcom the god of the children of Ammon, and have not walked in my ways, to do *that which is* right in mine eyes, and *to keep* my statutes and my judgments, as *did* David his father. 34 Howbeit I will not take the whole kingdom out of his hand: but I will make him prince all the days of his life for David my servant's sake, whom I chose, because he kept my commandments and my statutes: 35 But I will take the kingdom out of his son's hand, and will give it unto thee, *even* ten tribes. 36 And unto his son will I give one tribe, that David my servant may have a light alway before me in Jerusalem, the city which I have chosen me to put my name there.

37 And I will take thee, and thou shalt reign according to all that thy soul desireth, and shalt be king over Israel. 38 And it shall be, if thou wilt hearken unto all that I command thee, and wilt walk in my ways, and do *that is* right in my sight, to keep my statutes and my commandments, as David my servant did; that I will be with thee, and build thee a sure house, as I built for David, and will give Israel unto thee. 39 And I will for this afflict the seed of David, but not for ever."

This scripture reveals God's heart towards Israel, the matter at hand, being idolatry, and the terrible consequences of that idolatry. It clearly defines the "who, when, why and how" of the division of the nation of Israel in First Covenant days, leaving us no doubt or need for speculation. (See chart on the next page.)

LESSONS TO LEARN FROM THIS DIVISION
As we look at Israel, the division of that nation, and God's call to her to return to Him, there are numerous lessons the bible student gleans that are pertinent to our topic of Revival. One major lesson is God's call to His People to honour Him, above all things in their life.

Any follower of God, First or New Covenant, must always have God as their first love!

THE WHO, WHEN, WHY AND HOW OF THE DIVISION OF ISRAEL	
WHO	• God caused the division
WHEN	• After King Solomon's death in the time of his son, Rehoboam
WHY	• They forsook their God • They worshipped other gods: (Ashtoreth, Chemosh, Milcom) • They did not walk in God's Ways • They did not do that which was right in God's eyes
HOW	• God split the nation of Israel between two leaders: • Rehoboam, Solomon's Son, and • Jeroboam, a respected leader in the nation.

The following scriptures reaffirm this:

Exodus 20:2-3 2 I am YeHoVaH thy God, which have brought thee out of the land of Egypt, out of the house of bondage. 3 Thou shalt have no other gods before me.

Deuteronomy 6:5	5 And thou shalt love YeHoVaH thy God with all thine heart, and with all thy soul, and with all thy might.
Deuteronomy 11:1	Therefore thou shalt love YeHoVaH thy God, and keep his charge, and his statutes, and his judgments, and his commandments, alway.

The Apostolic writings of Matthew, Mark and Luke saw fit to record Yeshua's teaching on the same subject:

Matthew 22:37	Jesus said unto him, Thou shalt love YeHoVaH thy God with all thy heart, and with all thy soul, and with all thy mind.
Mark 12:30	And thou shalt love YeHoVaH thy God with all thy heart, and with all thy soul, and with all thy mind, and with all thy strength: this is the first commandment.
Luke 10:27	And he answering said, Thou shalt love YeHoVaH thy God with all thy heart, and with all thy soul, and with all thy strength, and with all thy mind; and thy neighbour as thyself.

It is obvious, by these quotes from both Hebraic and Apostolic scriptures, God requires, and deserves, no other place in our life but first. We, like the people of God living under the Covenant with God in ancient Israel, must love God with all our heart, mind, soul and strength. Not to do so, positions us, as it positioned Israel, to hear the same words God spoke to Northern Israel in Hosea 6: "Come and let us return unto YeHoVaH".

PERSONAL REFLECTION[5]

Take these scriptures on the previous page and spend some time with YeHoVaH. Ask Him if you have anything or anyone that you might place before Him in your life. Write down what you think He tells you, and then, with His help, develop a personal plan to remedy the situation.

THE DIVIDED KINGDOM

Looking back at Northern Israel, we know it was never God's intentions for the people within that nation to abandon Him, nor His Laws and practices of

---

[5] In this book you will find *a few* headings labeled, "Personal Reflection". There are only 4 of them put in some strategic areas of thought, however, not in every area where reflection might occur. Do take the time and reflect on any part of this book that touches your heart. You can only find blessing in doing so!

instruction, given by Moses, to the whole nation of Israel. Jeroboam, however, even though promised a prosperous kingdom, had his own unique ideas on how 'his kingdom' might prosper.

Unfortunately, those plans conflicted with the plans of God for the firm establishment of Northern Israel. Earlier, before Jeroboam began his reign, as you read in 1 Kings 11:34-39, Northern Israel never had a separate throne, and the revelation to do so only came when God carefully presented, in love, His specific plan for Northern Israel, to Jeroboam. These plans were neither ambiguous, nor confusing, yet Jeroboam and his counselors ignored them. Their rebellious attitude led to a rebellious leadership, which eventually corrupted Northern Israel.

The chart on the next page summarizes God's plans for Judah, and Northern Israel. It outlines the special conditions required of Jeroboam *if* he was to receive the promises; and, show the promised result including the length of time God planned to afflict Judah. (see Chart: The Specifics of God's Plan).

Historical evidence as well as biblical evidence,[6] tells us that the people of the North crowned Jeroboam as

---

[6] Read about the situation in detail in 1 Kings 12:1-24

THE SPECIFICS OF GOD'S PLAN	
JUDAH	<ul><li>Solomon's son made a prince for David's sake because King David kept God's commandments and statutes.</li><li>Take the kingdom (of Israel) out of the hand of Solomon's son (Rehoboam)</li></ul>
TRIBES: Judah, Benjamin, and the Levites.	
NORTHERN ISRAEL	<ul><li>Take ten tribes and give them to Jeroboam</li><li>Make Jeroboam King over Israel</li></ul>
TRIBES: Reuben, Simeon, Zebulun, Issachar, Dan, Gad, Asher, Naphtali, Ephraim, Manasseh.	

THE CONDITIONS FOR JEROBOAM

- Listen to all God commands him
- Walk in God's ways
- Do that which is right in God's eyes
- Keep God's statutes and commands

PROMISED RESULT

- Jeroboam reigns as his heart desired
- God is with him
- God builds Jeroboam a sure house as He built for David
- Israel given to Jeroboam

HOW LONG WILL GOD AFFLICT JUDAH?

- David's seed afflicted but not for ever

their King, and immediately after, civil war between the North and the South threatened to break out. Israel's original King in the South, Rehoboam, gathered his army to fight Jeroboam and his supporters in the North, to squash what he perceived as rebellion against him, and he wanted to regain the territory that once belonged to the kingdom of Judah. Into that heated situation, God sent a prophet to speak to Rehoboam, King of the South. As the prophet reiterated God's plan for the division, Rehoboam listened to YeHoVaH and left off all plans for civil war with the North. Even though divided, the nation remained at peace, now with two kings.

After the dissolution of Rehoboam's plans for civil war, Jeroboam began to implement plans that he felt would give strength to the North. He built a capital for his nation in Shechem, the original place where Rehoboam earlier desired the people to crown him king.[7] There, Jeroboam built the capital of Northern Israel and, there, he firmly established the throne of Northern Israel to stand throughout the nation's existence.

Yet, for all his endeavours to strengthen his kingdom, Jeroboam never grasped the need to fulfill the necessary requirements by God to keep him and his

---

[7] 1 Kings 12:1

seed upon the throne [8]. This failure, to keep YeHoVaH's conditions, meant Jeroboam nullified the promises. Let's recap them:

RECAP OF JEROBOAM'S FAILURE TO KEEP YEHOVAH'S COMMANDS:	
Reference	Jeroboam's behaviour
1 Kings 12: 26	• Jeroboam said in his heart, the kingdom shall return to David *(thus showing he did not trust YeHoVaH to keep His word to give Jeroboam those tribes)*
1 Kings 12: 26-27	• Jeroboam knew that God commanded worship at the temple *in Jerusalem*, which was located in Judah. He feared the people, following God's command to worship in Jerusalem, would choose the land of Judah, which housed God's Temple, over the land of the North, which, at that time, had no temple. • Jeroboam further feared that the people's loyalty would automatically fall to Judah's King, Rehoboam, forsaking him.

---

[8] 1 Kings 22:26-33

1 Kings 12: 28-32	• Jeroboam, when trying to resolve what he perceived as a problem, received, and then heeded bad counsel, taking the word of his counsellors above the Word of God personally given to him. From the implementation of that counsel, Jeroboam did the following: • Built two golden calves as idols • Located these golden calves in Dan and Bethel (*Bethel was already a religious site where at one time the Ark and the tabernacle of Moses stood*) • Said to Israel, it is too hard for you to go to Jerusalem to worship, so worship *these gods*, for these brought you out of Egypt • Made a temple, with altars, in both of these places and offered. • sacrifices to the golden calves • Made priests of the lowest of people but not of the tribe of Levi as God specified through Moses. • Ordained a feast, like the Feast of Tabernacles celebrating the harvest.

NORTHERN ISRAEL'S UNFAITHFULNESS

Unfortunately, all Northern Israel followed Jeroboam's new system of worship, as did the many kings who succeeded Jeroboam. A search through the bible shows that, in God's eyes, Northern Israel, from its beginning under Jeroboam, until its last king, Hoshea, never enjoyed even one good king to sit upon their throne. Not one had a heart for God like King David.

In addition, and perhaps more pertinent to our topic of revival, the bible does not record one 'revival' in Northern Israel. While God called them to return to Him and to put away their idolatry, the request went unanswered. Northern Israel continued in a downward spiral worshipping false gods and doing their own thing. Eventually, God removed Northern Israel from His Sight, scattering them from their homeland, and thus, He eliminated their abominable practices of idolatry from His sight.

HOSEA'S TIME

When Hosea came on the scene and spoke God's invitation for Revival, it was prior to Northern Israel's dispersal, and voiced in the hopes of avoiding it. Unfortunately, Hosea's words from God did not break through the blatantly disobedient hearts of the people for they were so deeply bedded in idolatry, and happy with that choice, they did not even entertain thoughts of change. After all, their leaders, including the King, lived as they did, following their faith as did generations before them.

Former Prophets sent to Northern Israel to break through the idolatry, normally met strong resistance for change, but God's plan with Hosea was different. In a strategic effort to break the crust of the hardened hearts of His People, Hosea displayed God's viewpoint, in circumstances, through his own life. *Through the life of the prophet, Hosea, God showed Himself as a husband to Israel, and showed Israel as His adulterous wife.*

When we arrive at Hosea Chapter 6, (our opening scripture) Hosea's career in *sign prophecy* [9] and prophetic utterance was well underway. Out of the depths of mercy and compassion, comes the cry of revival, the call, as YeHoVaH speaks to Northern Israel through His prophet:

1 **Come**, and let us **return** unto YeHoVaH: for he hath **torn**, and he will **heal** us; he hath **smitten**, and he will **bind** us up. 2 After two days will he **revive us**: in the third day he will **raise** us up, and we shall **live** in his **sight**. 3 Then shall

---

[9] A SIGN PROPHET is a person assigned by God to speak to people by demonstrating the Word of God with their own life, and/or with other things that strongly portray God's plans and purposes.

*we **know**, if we **follow on** to know YeHoVaH: his **going forth** is prepared as the morning; and he shall **come** unto us as the **rain**, as the latter and former rain unto the earth.* Hosea 6:1-3

Throughout the book, as we continue to look further into this scripture, we will gain a good understanding of the amazing promises God, in His love and mercy, gave to a stubborn, rebellious, and hard-hearted people. In this chapter, we will begin to unlock the marvellous truths in this scripture passage by looking at three words interpreted into English as "*come, live and revive*".

Examining these words in the original Hebrew picture language, will enlighten us to the scripture's meaning.

THE ANCIENT HEBREW PICTURE LANGUAGE
Whenever you translate something from one language to another, there is always a risk of compromising the depth of the original language, especially if that language is not as expressive as the original, and does not hold words, which precisely articulate the meaning. Such is the case when translating from Hebrew to English.

For example, to translate a Hebrew 'tallit', which is an important part of the traditional Jewish garment, worn by men, we have no such English word to express it. The word 'tallit' means little tent but the translators simply interpreted it, as 'tent'. In our language, however, when we think of a tent, we know there are large tents and pup tents. However, 'tallit', if properly interpreted, is, in reality, a woven shawl traditionally made on a white background, in which people wrap themselves when they are alone in prayer with God. Today we call that a prayer shawl. Translating the word, 'tallit' as 'tent', hardly means the same thing.

This is but one instance where early interpretations of scripture erred, and because of that one little mistake, many believers think that Acts 18:3, that described the Apostle Paul as abiding with 'tentmakers', means that Paul made tents, meaning outdoor shelters, when in fact, as a trained Pharisee, Paul made 'prayer shawls'. This is but one instance but there are many other places in the Word, where translators overlooked cultural expressions and the like, and thus, gave the reader a different meaning than the original transcripts.

We must always ensure, when looking at Hebrew words with our English mind, that we consider these things and remember that **Hebraic thinking differs greatly from our Western world.** Differences in thinking, between Hebraic and Western thought, would take a lot of time to explain, so for now, keep in mind, that the Hebraic language is 'relational' while the Western World is not. The Hebrew picture language explains that point well.

AN AGRICULTURAL BASED LANGUAGE
The early Hebrew language, like other languages, began as an *agriculturally based language* explaining ideas of their civilization with 'pictures' relative to their environment. The alphabet, in this early language, was comprised of letters, whose design indicated certain parts of the body to describe certain words.

Other letters used well-known animals such as the ox and others to describe common things during their civilization's existence. For example, the letter "aleph", the first letter pictured an ox's head, and the second letter "bet" represented a tent where the family lived. [10] To explain this in further detail, we will look at the word, "father", which uses both the "aleph" and the "bet".

THE HEBREW WORD FOR FATHER
Hebrew words usually have a base of three characters. The first two characters are known as Parent Root, the

---

[10] In the seminar, this is explained in greater detail. If you are using this material as a seminar, feel free to look up some information online as many people speak of this today.

characters following are known as the Child Root. [11] The word for father is Ab. In both English and Hebrew, it consists of two major letters. In English, the letters are A and B. In the Hebrew they are ALEPH and BET.

In English, we read this way:
from **Left to Right**: ⟶

In Hebrew, we read this way: ◀······················
from **Right to Left:**

For those who normally read in English, this seems awkward, but nevertheless keep that in mind as you read the letters below.

◀······················

בּ א

BET   ALEPH

In the picture language, an Ox's head represents the Aleph, and the Bet is pictured as a dwelling place, or a tent. The **ox** is a strong animal used to pull carts and carry heavy burdens and the like. Within a tent, the family lived. Putting this together, you have a picture

---

[11] When understanding "Parent and Child Root" it is only in the most simplistic format that it is easy to interpret. Past four or five characters, it is more difficult to grasp.

of a strong person capable of carrying burdens, caring for the family. Hence, the Hebrew picture language describes the father as this: *The strong person over the family, or to put it another way, a father is the strong one of the house.*

PERSONAL REFLECTION

In a spiritual application, our Heavenly Father is One who carries our burdens and cares for every person in the family, forgetting none. **Do you see your Heavenly Father in that light?** Take some time, pray about that, then try to remember that awesome picture of Him, and do cast all your care upon Him, for He cares for you.

1 Peter 5: 7

HEBREW WORDS IN HOSEA 6:1-3

There are 2 Hebrew words used in the original Hebrew language, however, interpreters used the English word, "come" in Hebrew. Exploring the 2 original Hebrew words, will give us a deeper understanding of Hosea 6:1-3 (refer to 16 to reread that text).

COME (vs 1) יְלָךְ	Pronounced yaw-lak	Strong's # 3212

OVERALL ORIGINAL WORD PICTURE MEANING:
This word picture indicates a call to walk forward towards someone to receive a blessing, or a gift from God's Divine Power.

The second word implies something slightly different.

COME (vs 3) בוא	pronounced bo	Strong's # 0935
OVERALL ORIGINAL WORD PICTURE MEANING:		
This word picture suggests a drawing near, confidently, and from that coming, there results an attachment and togetherness.		

The first word shows *the calling*, "to come", while the second word refers to a powerful, engaging contact with God, as He draws near to His People with mighty deeds and power. Sandwiched between the first and second use of the word interpreted, in English, as come, are two verses containing much meaning, the bulk of which requires repentance to obtain. These indicate that the result of a full return to God is an intimate knowledge of YeHoVaH, formerly unknown. We will see that later as we look deeper into the remaining Hebrew words.

Turning now to the word interpreted "revive" in verse 2, we read, "After two days, He will revive us: ..." The word for 'revive' is also the same word often interpreted as "life" or "live".

REVIVE (Also interpreted as **Life or Live**) חיה	Pronounced khaw-yaw	**Strong's # 2421**
OVERALL WORD PICTURE MEANING:		
This word pictures indicates a separation, or a wall erected to keep out anything that removes "breath" or "life". In a truly spiritual sense, true *life* is being full of God's Breath. To revive, then, is a process of walling out what removed life, and then replace whatever "life" ebbed away.		

Genesis 2:7 proves this point, that breath and life are connected:

THE BREATH OF LIFE
And YeHoVaH God formed man of the dust of the ground, and breathed into his nostrils the breath of life; and man became a living soul. Genesis 2:7

Many commentators on this verse agree it should translate: *"And YeHoVaH God formed man of the dust of the ground, and breathed into his nostrils the breath of* **lives**,

and man became a living soul." This plural form shows that God gave plural lives to humankind:
- A physical life
- A life of the soul (emotion, mind, will, etc)
- A spiritual life

If you continue to read about this word, חיה (pronounced "khaw-yaw") in a concordance you will find words such as revived, quickened, free from sickness, free from discouragement, free from faintness, and free from death.

In other words, to have life is to "wall out" sickness (sickness brings "death" to certain parts of the body); "wall out" discouragement (downcast spirit or spirit of heaviness); "wall out" faintness (to faint is to pale or weaken and then fall); "wall out" any form of death (which of course, ends all life).

> *In a truly biblical sense then, one is 'fully alive' when they are 'whole', free from things that cause them to 'die' in one way or another. In other words, the things that cause 'death' are walled out, not permitted in.*

Let's look at some scriptures to show this point:

Genesis 20:1-7

"1   And Abraham journeyed from thence toward the south country, and dwelled between Kadesh and Shur, and sojourned in Gerar. 2   And Abraham said of Sarah his wife, She *is* my sister: and Abimelech king of Gerar sent, and took Sarah. 3 ¶   But God came to Abimelech in a dream by night, and said to him, Behold, thou *art but* a dead man, for the woman which thou hast taken; for she *is* a man's wife. 4 But Abimelech had not come near her: and he said, Lord, wilt thou slay also a righteous nation? 5 Said he not unto me, She *is* my sister? and she, even she herself said, He *is* my brother: in the integrity of my heart and innocency of my hands have I done this. 6   And God said unto him in a dream, Yea, I know that thou didst this in the integrity of thy heart; for I also withheld thee from sinning against me: therefore suffered I thee not to touch her. 7   Now therefore restore the man *his* wife; for he *is* a prophet, and he shall pray for thee, and thou shalt <u>live:</u> <היה "khaw-yaw">. and if thou restore *her* not, know thou that thou shalt surely die, thou, and all that *are* thine."

God made His message to Abimelech clear. If Abimelech keeps Sarah, he would die, however, if Abimelech's actions culminated in returning Abraham his wife, then the consequence, of taking Sarah, which was his death, God would wall out and the man would remain alive.

Next, we'll look at two more examples of < היה "khaw-yaw"> which add to the clarity of the Hebrew Word Picture meaning.

Psalm 85:1-7 1 To the chief Musician, A Psalm for the sons of Korah.» YEHOVAH, thou hast been favourable unto thy land: thou hast brought back the captivity of Jacob. 2 Thou hast forgiven the iniquity of thy people, thou hast covered all their sin. Selah. 3 Thou hast taken away all thy wrath: thou hast turned thyself from the fierceness of thine anger. 4 Turn us, O God of our salvation, and cause thine anger toward us to cease. 5 Wilt thou be angry with us for ever? wilt thou draw out thine היה anger to all generations? 6 Wilt thou not **revive** < "khaw-yaw"> us again: that thy people may rejoice in thee? 7 Shew us thy mercy, O YEHOVAH, and grant us thy salvation.

Here the Psalmist reflects on the forgiveness of God to the children of Jacob. With all 'wrath' removed then the fierce anger turns away. There is a plea to turn the people's face once again towards God and then he petitions God to revive them.

Later on when we look at the word **'return'** this passage will hold greater meaning, but for now make note that, the people enjoyed *reviving* when God *walled out* 'wrath' and 'anger'. The Psalmist ends with a plea to grant salvation, which comes from God's mercy, a mercy that brings to a halt the well-deserved results.

> Psalm 138:7-8
> 7 Though I walk in the midst of trouble, thou wilt *revive* < "khaw-yaw"> חיה me: thou shalt stretch forth thine hand against the wrath of mine enemies, and thy right hand shall save me. 8 YeHoVaH will perfect that which concerneth me: thy mercy, O YEHOVAH, endureth for ever: forsake not the works of thine own hands.

This petitions God for a "reviving", while in the midst of trouble. Surely, God stretching forth His Hand towards the wrath of the enemy threatening destroy them, constitutes a "walling out" or "blocking out" and thus ending that which promised injury to God's people. This passage, and many other Hebraic passages, clearly describe, "Reviving", in this capacity.

NEW COVENANT WRITINGS

Within the Apostolic Scriptures, translators interpreted the Greek text with the word "revived" in only two places. The first place is in the book of Romans:

Romans 7:9   9 *"For I was alive without the law once: but when the commandment came, sin revived, and I died."*

The Greek Word interpreted "revived", means "to be alive again", but here the topic is 'sin', and obviously, does not refer to Revival in the way we speak of it today.

The second place in which interpreters used the word "revive" is:

Romans 14:9   9 For to this end Christ both died, and rose, and *revived*, that he might be Lord both of the dead and living.

This scripture is a clear reference to the Resurrection of Messiah, and its use here, as in the Hebraic scripture, shows that God walled out "death" from Yeshua's crucified body. To emphasize that death's removal, one Apostolic writer penned, "O death, where is your sting? O grave, where is your victory[12]?"

These are all the scriptures, within the New Covenant, which use the word, "revived". There is another scripture, which comes close to implying revival, but, to keep things simple, we will look at that later. At this point, we will conclude by identifying the call of Revival, and describe it from an Hebraic perspective.

REVIVAL'S CALL	
Its Message (from Hosea 6: 1)	"Come and "Return" to YeHoVaH (our Covenant God)
Its Hebraic Perspective (from Hosea 6:2)	Allow the Holy Spirit to wall out "death", to keep out anything that takes away "life".

Keep in mind, it is a call to RETURN, the meaning of which we will look at in another lesson.

---

[12] 1 Corinthians 15:55 O death, where is thy sting? O grave, where is thy victory? Romans 14:9

REVIVAL'S PROMISE 2

Continuing with our word study in Hosea 6:1-3, please refresh your mind with this scripture regarding revival:

*Come, and let us **return** unto YeHoVaH: for he hath **torn**, and he will **heal** us; he hath **smitten**, and he will **bind** us up. 2 After two days will he **revive** us: in the third day he will **raise** us up, and we shall **live** in his **sight**. 3 Then shall we **know**, if we **follow on** to **know** YeHoVaH: his **going forth** is prepared as the morning; and he shall **come** unto us as the **rain**, as the latter and former **rain** unto the earth.*

Hosea 6: 1-3

In this section, we will look at the following words:

| Return | YEHOVAH | Torn |
| Heal | Smitten | Bind |

Again, we will look at the original Hebrew words in the Pictograph language, since this gives us a much clearer idea of what the initial Hebrew word implies.

RETURN שׁוּב	Pronounced shoob	Strong's # 7725
OVERALL WORD PICTURE MEANING:		
This word picture indicates a destruction of the things attached to a person. So, to return, in this sense, is to *turn away* from the things, whatever they might be, that kept you in its grasp. It means to turn to God, turning your back on what kept you away.		

When translating this word שׁוּב <7725>, in three places, translators inserted the word "repent" rather than "return". Those scriptures are as follows:

1 Kings 8: 47-48
47 Yet if they shall bethink themselves in the land whither they were carried captives, and **repent <07725>,** and make supplication unto thee in the land of them that carried them captives, saying, We have sinned, and have done perversely, we have committed wickedness; 48 And so **return <07725>,** unto thee with all their heart, and with all their soul, in the

land of their enemies, which led them away captive, and pray unto thee toward their land, which thou gavest unto their fathers, the city which thou hast chosen, and the house which I have built for thy name:

Ezekiel 14:6 — 6 Therefore say unto the house of Israel, Thus saith YeHoVaH GOD; **Repent <07725>,** and turn yourselves from your idols; and turn away your faces from all your abominations.

Ezekiel 18:30 — 30 Therefore I will judge you, O house of Israel, every one according to his ways, saith YeHoVaH GOD. **Repent <07725>,** and turn yourselves from all your transgressions; so iniquity shall not be your ruin.

You can see from these previous three scriptures, that the word repent fits nicely into the context of the passage, and it strongly suggests *a turning* away. In recap, please note that:

- 1 Kings 8:47 comes from the prayer of Solomon when he dedicated the Temple. In this case, Solomon asks for a people who will *turn away* from the idolatry, and other things, that took them away from God. Ezekiel 14:6 relates a call of God to His People to leave behind, or *turn away* from idolatry.

- Ezekiel 18:30 speaks of another call for God's People to *turn away* from transgressions and iniquity so these things will not be their destruction.

These three scriptures clearly show the connection of *turning away* from whatever grabbed them and took them away from God. With that thought in mind, there is one more scripture to look at which shows us another important factor of the word "return".

| Malachi 3: 7 | 7 Even from the days of your fathers ye are gone away from mine ordinances, and have not kept them. **Return** <07725>, unto me, and I will **return** <07725>, unto you, saith YeHoVaH of hosts. But ye said, Wherein shall we return? <07725>, |

As you read this scripture, note God calls the people to return to Him, meaning, "turn away from whatever took you away from God", and then God says, "I will return to you", meaning 'I will *turn away* from whatever took Me away from you". To understand that thought clearly, we must remember that under the First Covenant, when the people sinned and after many warnings, refused to repent, then God looked away from the people.

Malachi 3:7 promises that if God's People remove what took ***them*** away from ***Him***, then He will remove what took ***Him*** away from ***them***, namely sin.

In other words:

God receives His People's repentance, which, under the First Covenant system, meant an accompanying sin offering.

God then puts out of His Sight, the "sin" that caused them to forsake Him and initiated the cause for Him to look away from them until they repented.

Looking back under the First Covenant system then, Revival came when God's people obeyed the call of God to ***Return to Him***. The people removed what pulled them away from God, and God removed whatever offended Him, namely their sin.

Was that the point at which the people could then expect the promised revival?

Let's read the passage again:

> *Hosea 6:1-2*   1 Come, and let us **return** unto YeHoVaH: for he hath torn, and he will heal us; he hath smitten, and he will bind us up. 2 **After two days will he revive us**: in the third day he will raise us up, and we shall live in his sight.

The two days here refers to the time of their affliction mentioned in verse 1.

Reflecting upon the word, "return", we see that God called them to "remove what took them away from Him", after which, He revives them. This means *revival's entrance depends upon the willingness of God's people to 'put away their sin'*.

As we explore the topic of Revival further, you will soon discover this pattern in Hosea is not an isolated example. "Return to Me and I will return to you", is a continuous theme running continuously throughout the Hebraic scriptures.

Thus far, you have seen it in Malachi, the book of Kings, Ezekiel and, in the very root of the word שׁוּב <07725> 'return'. The theme is virtually in the background of every plea of God to His People, who wandered away from the truth.

BACK TO NORTHERN ISRAEL

Unfortunately, Northern Israel never returned to God. Scripture, therefore, had no opportunity to speak of these people as a revived entity that returned to God, but rather, paints a picture of an idolatrous people, and a cruel and ruthless government in Northern Israel, living far away from God. In speaking of their last king, Hoshea, scripture relates how he murdered the previous, reigning king and sat himself upon the throne. [13]This was not the first time a King in Northern Israel was murdered, either. In fact, Hosea refers to this very issue when he says:

> Hosea 8:4   4 "They have set up kings, but not by me: they have made princes, and I knew it not: of their silver and their gold have they made them idols that they may be cut off."

All of this shows the great wickedness and total lack of repentance within Northern Israel. We can rightly conclude that the majority of people, within that nation, never turned away from their offences to God, and consequently, did not realize the promised Revival.

---

[13] 2 Kings 15:29-3

PERSONAL REFLECTION

First Covenant people needed to repent for their sins. Likewise, so do believers *if they live their live contrary to scripture.* Take some time. Seek God's face to see if your life has areas which offend God. If so, this indicates a need to turn away from those things offensive to Him. Ask His help to remain open to hear His Voice in this regard, as it is possible that He may perceive things in His eyes, differently than you presently realize.

RETURNING TO HOSEA 6:1-3

To continue in our understanding of this scripture, we will look at the word the original Hebrew word for "LORD"[14].

(Refer to chart on the next page.)

---

[14] Many know that the name of YHVH was not pronounced except by the priest once a year, but some do not know that particular practise did not happen for centuries after Hosea. It was not until the captives of Judah returned from Babylon and resettled in the land that this bann on the name came into force.

LORD: יהוה	Pronunciation YeHoVaH	Strong's # 3068

OVERALL WORD PICTURE MEANING:
Due to the complexity of this word, we will look at each letter. י "yod": This letter suggests works, deeds, with God's Hand outstretched to perform them ה "heh": this letter strongly suggests *the presence of God's breath, or **His Spirit*** and further suggests an awesome thing These above two letters structure what we call the 'parent root'. The next two letters make up the child root. ו "vav": suggests an attachment, something joining one to another such as in a covenant relationship ה "heh" suggests once more, the presence of God's breath, something wonderful and it can mean a victory
The usual interpretation of this word is that God exists on His Own. You can see this in the Picture, as His own breath sustains Him and you can see further that the work of God's Breath, which is mighty, attaches itself and brings whatever is needed for victory by His Spirit. (The attachment clearly shows the idea of covenant.)

> To add the name to another such as "Shalom" or "Rapha", you have: "The work of the *His Spirit* (His Breath) establishes peace, or healing, etc." (Again, keep in mind the covenant relationship.)

Keep in mind the following:

- The strong thoughts of covenant within this name shows that God is a covenant keeping God, and those in covenant with Him can expect great things from Him.
- Residing in this meaning rests a strong implication that God can do "any work" or "anything" needed, *and* it is done by His Breath, His Spirit, (e.g. miracles, healings, victory in battle and the like.)
- **He is the Victorious One Who overcomes all things!**

> IN SUMMARY, we could say the Hebrew word we interpret as YEHOVAH <יהוה> shows a picture of the Covenant God (of Israel), Who promised to walk with His People, doing wonders, on their behalf, making them victorious.

The Prophets of God knew these aspects of His character as conveyed by the picture language. Many scriptures, too numerous to mention, indicate that fact.

Below are just a few examples:

Genesis 15:7	7 And he said unto him, I am YeHoVaH <יהוה> that brought thee out of Ur of the Chaldees, to give thee this land to inherit it.
Isaiah 44:24	24 Thus saith YeHoVaH, thy redeemer, and he that formed thee from the womb, I am YeHoVaH <יהוה> that maketh all things; that stretcheth forth the heavens alone; that spreadeth abroad the earth by myself;
Isaiah 48:17	17 Thus saith YeHoVaH <יהוה>, thy Redeemer, the Holy One of Israel; I am YeHoVaH <יהוה> thy God which teacheth thee to profit, which leadeth thee by the way that thou shouldest go.
Isaiah 51:15	15 But I am YeHoVaH <יהוה> thy God that divided the sea, whose waves roared: YeHoVaH of hosts is his name.

RECAP OF HOSEA 6:1-

These Hebrew Word pictures expand, or broaden the original meaning, giving us greater depth to the word, but the thing to remember is to *ensure all conclusions fit both the passage in question and other biblical passages on the same subject.*

Below is a recap of the English interpretation from the King James Version of the scriptures, and following that is a wide paraphrase using the information from the Hebrew Word pictures.

The English text reads:	Come, and let us return unto YeHoVaH
Hebrew Picture reads:	Draw near to God for a blessing from His Divine Power. Turn your backs on whatever things have kept you away from Him. Turn to the One Who promised to walk with you, doing wonders on your behalf making you victorious.

Does this expanded or wide paraphrase still hold within biblical context?

| Genesis 49:25 | 25 Even by the God of thy father, who shall help thee; and by the Almighty, who shall bless thee with blessings of heaven above, blessings of the deep that lieth under, blessings of the breasts, and of the womb: |

Here we see that the Almighty is the One who gives blessings, so this conclusion is correct.

| Joshua 24:14 | 14 Now therefore fear YeHoVaH, and serve him in sincerity and in truth: and put away the gods, which your fathers served on the other side of the flood, and in Egypt; and serve ye YeHoVaH. |

Joshua's words confirm the need to put away, or turn your back on anything offensive to God.

| Exodus 29:46 | 46 And they shall know that I am YeHoVaH their God, that brought them forth out of the land of Egypt, that I may dwell among them: I am YeHoVaH their God. |

Here, God makes it very clear that He is not only walking with them, but He lives in the midst of His People.

1 Chronicles 29:11	11 "Thine, O YEHOVAH, [is] the greatness, and the power, and the glory, and the victory, and the majesty: for all [that is] in the heaven and in the earth [is thine]; thine [is] the kingdom, O YEHOVAH, and thou art exalted as head above all."

This is but one of the hundreds of passages proving God is an awesome God, doing wonders and giving His people victory.

These scriptures, and more besides, support the conclusions drawn from the Hebrew word pictures, and these conclusions do fit into the verse context, more of which we will see later.

We can be comfortable with this thus far, however, with every word picture, we must be careful *to continue to align with the whole counsel of God.* Our goal is *never to re-write any biblical passage*, but rather to gain a deeper understanding of the original text.

With this in mind, let us continue to see the deeper meanings of the words in our text, in Hosea 6:1, by looking at the word "heal".

HEAL:	2 possible roots both pronounced raw-faw	Strong's # 7495
רפא רפה		

OVERALL WORD PICTURE MEANING:

Both root words share the same parent root, or 1st two letters:

ר   "resh": this letter pictures the beginning, the top of, or head of

פ   "pey": this letter pictures a mouth, or what comes from the mouth which is 'words'.

These above two letters, structuring the 'parent root', indicate the superior word, or the ultimate Word.

א   "aleph" the one child root, means pulling into order, or strength, or carrying burdens

This makes the first word shows רפא a picture of the Ultimate or highest word comes and puts things in order or bears the burdens and thus it brings healing.

The second word רפה uses:

ה   "heh" suggests the presence of God's breath, something wonderful, a Victory.

This makes the second word show a picture of the Ultimate Word comes by the Spirit of God.

> **SUMMARY:** In both these words, we have a picture of the Word of God as an important part of healing:
> - Surely, he hath borne our griefs, and carried our sorrows: yet be esteemed him stricken, smitten of God, and afflicted. Isaiah 53: 4
> - He sent His Word and healed them. Psalm
> - 107:20

To bring home the specific promised 'healing' to Northern Israel, we must first look at the word, **"torn"**, since the poetic language in Hosea suggests a strong connection between the two Hebrew words: torn and heal.

TORN טרף	Pronounced taw-raf	**Strong's # 2963**
OVERALL WORD PICTURE MEANING:		
This word pictures indicates 'to surround something, to bring in a rulership, which will scatter or weaken something'. It means to set a snare, and thus, as head over what one snared, it scatters it. It means to surround, then rule and tear into pieces.		
COMMENTS: The use of the English word 'torn' is good, since it means to see something whole, ripped or shredded. In that sense, something, once whole, becomes fragmented. However, our word "torn" leaves out the sense of surrounding and ruling.		

THE REASON FOR THE TEARING

In looking at this word, שׂרה interpreted as "torn", we cannot overlook the first letter ט "tet". This letter suggests something hidden, something enclosed. In the action of 'tearing' something open, that feat 'breaks open' the thing hidden thus revealing what is on the inside. Looking at this from another viewpoint, something hidden is not naked to the eye, and therefore when one looks at the object, *they see one thing*, when in reality *it is another*. This is a form of deception.

With that thought *of deception* in mind, you can see that as Northern Israel looked at the faith they practiced, they saw the *external side of that faith*, believing it to be the faith of their forefathers. Due to Jeroboam's trickery, they had a religion with certain similarities, but without the truth at its heart. They practised one thing, which, in truth, was something else. They were deceived.

Even though YeHoVaH sent some mighty prophets, such as Elijah and Elisha, to break the deception, few responded. For the most part, Northern Israel did not turn away from their counterfeit faith and generations into the deception, these people remained in darkness, holding to the faith Jeroboam established. In order to forsake their error, their actions proved they needed more than the voice of God's prophets.

One might wonder why the mighty prophets of God did not break through the minds of those caught in deception. One reason was that the false prophets, within that *system of faith,* kept the people in darkness. Their prominent voices assured the people that they were not in any danger from God. Unfortunately, the people believed the false prophets, since their message was more appealing than the message of God's true prophets.

Another reason for resistance to God's true prophets came from the leadership, within the nation. *The governmental rulership of Northern Israel, from its inception, rested upon the same erroneous faith and its practices established by Jeroboam.* Their powerful influence added to the circumstances to keep the deception operative.

This system then, with all its false prophets and governmental leaders, including the King, and all things that lay behind the scene, *was the target of God's strike*. The goal of God's strike was to expose the deception by the use of economic difficulties, drought, blight, crop failure and the like. This should turn the people back to God having shown them it inadequacies of their false faith, for their false gods could not change the circumstances, but the true God could. With the deception of their false gods, exposed,

Israel then could make a choice, namely, "Whom would they serve?"

As the people of Northern Israel made their choice, most listened to the voice of the false prophets who interpreted the current events of the nation in a different way than the true prophets, and thus, the bulk of the people continued to serve the false religious system they practiced for generations.

In the end, the true Prophets of God met with stronger and stronger resistance and since we know God scattered Northern Israel, we know the prophetic words only chipped away at the outer edge of the system. One of their last prophets to speak to them was none other than the prophet Hosea, who cried out for repentance before enormous trouble came to Northern Israel. Unfortunately, Hosea's voice, like the prophets before him, went unheeded.

When God finally gave the false religious system its deathblow, the whole nation fell apart. Suddenly, the people faced the stark and painful reality that God's true prophets predicted. In their enslavement to Assyria and their scattering to the ends of the earth, that generation would have good reason to forsake the false system of worship that led them to such destruction, but the question remains, did they do so?

Only heaven, however, will reveal such details about the generation left alive when the deathblow finally came to Northern Israel. As its people became the captives of Assyria, and many scattered to the ends of the earth, we can learn from their stubbornness and apply it to our own situations.

In addition, in our day, as we see the exiles returning to their own homeland of Israel, we surely can pray for these returnees to look to the true God with all their heart, mind, soul and strength, and in that, recognize their Saviour, Yeshua. Then, the healing waiting for them, promised so long before, through the lips of prophets, would find fulfillment in their lives.

A SHORT DETOUR

We understand then that God tore Northern Israel, to destroy *the counterfeit system of worship that* kept Israel in darkness. By scattering the components of that false system, *the system* would not rise again to lead more and more people into its deceptive pathway. One of those components God scattered, the false prophet, earlier acted like glue, keeping the system together. Let us take a sidestep then and look at *one aspect* of that system which kept Northern Israel in deception, namely, *the false prophet.*

While the scripture below speaks of Southern Israel, or Judah, the prophets of Northern Israel fit well into the same scenario.

Jeremiah 23: 18 For who hath stood in the counsel of YeHoVaH, and hath perceived and heard his word? who hath marked his word, and heard it? 19 Behold, a whirlwind of YeHoVaH is gone forth in fury, even a grievous whirlwind: it shall fall grievously upon the head of the wicked. 20 The anger of YeHoVaH shall not return, until he have executed, and till he have performed the thoughts of his heart: in the latter days ye shall consider it perfectly. 21 I have not sent these prophets, yet they ran: I have not spoken to them, yet they prophesied. 22 But if they had stood in my counsel, and had caused my people to hear my words, then they should have turned them from their evil way, and from the evil of their doings. 23 Am I a God at hand, saith YeHoVaH, and not a God afar off? 24 Can any hide himself in secret places that I shall not see him? saith YeHoVaH. Do not I fill heaven and earth? saith YeHoVaH.

25 I have heard what the prophets said, that prophesy lies in my name, saying, I have dreamed, I have dreamed. 26 How long shall this be in the heart of the prophets that prophesy lies? yea, they are prophets of the deceit of their own heart; 27 Which think to cause my people to forget my name by their dreams which they tell every man to his neighbour, as their fathers have forgotten my name for Baal.

Let's recap what this scripture conveys: *the problem with False Prophets.*

THE PROBLEM WITH FALSE PROPHETS [15]

The first, major problem, revealed in the previous scripture, is that false prophets do not stand in God's counsel and thus, do not perceive, nor hear God's Word. Yet, even without an assignment from the Almighty, the false prophet ran to vocalize his message to any listening ear. Consequently, since they were not God's choice to speak to His People to return to Him, false prophets usually add to the difficulty and instead, reinforced the error.

---

[15] This passaged gives us some of the problems with false prophets, but not all! Other scriptures elaborate further. Consider investigating on your own to discover more.

Jeremiah, in the passage you just read, makes it very clear, if the prophets, who went out to speak to the people, had spoken God's counsel, their words would *turn the people* from their wicked ways. Instead, these prophets, void of God's counsel, spoke from the deception of their own hearts, prophesying dreams and visions not from God. The result of these false prophets was a people who *forgot God's name* and ended up serving other gods.

Looking back at Northern Israel, the false prophets cultivated and continued to sow lies into their false system of worship. The problem intensified as the priests in Northern Israel, which were not from the tribe of Levi as God ordained, but rather of Jeroboam's choosing, did not teach the Laws of God, but rather led the people further and further into idol worship and sin.

Concisely recapped, the true faith, however, when followed, went like this: God taught His people, through Moses, how to present acceptable sacrifices to YeHoVaH and He gave established guidelines for behaviour towards God and humankind. Priests learned these things and then taught the people, so they could live a pleasing life before His Face. True prophets, God sent, called the people to return to God and obey His commands.

In Northern Israel, when Jeroboam shifted the priesthood, taught other behavioural guidelines, and replaced the acceptable sacrifices with others unacceptable, he created a rift between the people and God. Neither priest, nor false prophets sought to restore that broken relationship, but rather taught error, which of course, left a deceived people practising a perverse faith.

Jeroboam's faith system, based partly upon the system of Moses and partly upon a system of idolatry, pleased both Jeroboam and the people, but not God. You can hear the motive of Jeroboam and his people-pleasing attitude in the following scripture:

| 1 Kings 12:26-30 | 26 And Jeroboam said in his heart, Now shall the kingdom return to the house of David: 27 If this people go up to do sacrifice in the house of YeHoVaH at Jerusalem, then shall the heart of this people turn again unto their lord, even unto Rehoboam king of Judah, and they shall kill me, and go again to Rehoboam king of Judah. 28 Whereupon *__the king took counsel__*, and made *two calves of gold*, and said unto them, *It is too much for you to go up to Jerusalem: behold thy gods, O Israel, which brought* |

> *thee up out of the land of Egypt.* 29 And he set the one in Bethel, and the other put he in Dan. 30 And this thing became a sin: for the people went to worship before the one, even unto Dan. ***And he made an house of high places, and made priests of the lowest of the people, which were not of the sons of Levi.***

In this initial set up of their new worship system, Jeroboam presented this people-pleasing idea in order to save them from a tough journey to Jerusalem, a journey God gave to them to complete at certain times during the year, in order to bless them. Perhaps God insisted on this journey to Jerusalem to prove their hearts towards Him, and at the same time, embed the true faith into their hearts, as their determination arose to follow His command.

With the false faith followed by the people, Jeroboam put his fear to rest. Rather than trust in YeHoVaH's Promises to keep the people within the kingdom of Northern Israel, Jeroboam installed provisions to ensure the people's loyalty to him, caring not that he shifted the people to a false worship system. To keep the people near him in Northern Israel, he profaned and prostituted the faith.

NORTHERN ISRAEL'S FOUNDATION

As said earlier, the original problem with Northern Israel arose when Jeroboam introduced them to idolatry. This idolatry formed the foundation on which Northern Israel rested. By the time you arrive at Hosea's prophesies, it is nearly 200 years down the road from their early beginnings. The sins of Jeroboam, in which he caused Israel to sin, *never dissipated*. Generations of kings, religious leaders, and religious traditions continued until the belief system firmly entrenched itself within the hearts and minds of the people. This system, so familiar to them, felt right. *It emerged as the right thing to do.* The true prophets of God, who advocated the right ways of God, often appeared as dissenters.

Numerous true prophets went unheeded by the people and thus Northern Israel refused to forsake the earlier foundation Jeroboam built, even though it was corrupt and offensive to God. These people seemed locked into their way of doing things, and with their religious leaders and their king holding to those same ways, they could not see past their deception.

Northern Israel's religious deception made it hard for the people to break away, because ***it rested upon a wrong foundation, and did so, ever since the nation's inception.*** Even though error and idolatry formed their religious foundation, the bulk of the people, including priests, prophets, government leaders and kings, clung tight to it, based their life upon it, reared their children to obey it. In short, they built their entire national system upon a fake, phoney, non-reality.

God, in His mercy, as we said earlier, hit hard against that system, with the purpose of crumbling it to the ground. That blow, acting like a powerful earthquake, shattered the strength of the system. The King, government officials, priests, prophets, all adherents to the false faith, along with the entire nation, could no longer take refuge within that system.

Yes, this nation was TORN. As the Hebrew word picture suggests, YeHoVaH surrounded them, cracked open the deception and brought in a new rulership. For the people of Northern Israel in that day, it meant Assyria's rulership, which we know was hard and cruel.

Perhaps the words of Hosea and other prophets rang in the ears of some of the people of Northern Israel, as they left that land for another. For any captives that lived, repented and turned to Him, they, however, would have the true God's rulership amidst their circumstances. They would see His hand of mercy, yes, His promised healing awaited them. That was the hope in Hosea 6:1 to Hosea 6:3.

WHEN GOD TEARS

God tears to expose what His People do not see. As in Northern Israel, so too today, the "false", "fake", or "imitations" of the true, act as parallels to the truth, and over the years, hide behind traditions and the like. God tears, therefore, to expose what His People do not recognize as error. People, seeing the false thus exposed, must then make a choice to forsake the false or phony and embrace the truth, or keep the error.

WHAT DOES GOD'S TEARING LOOK LIKE?

In Northern Israel, as we saw earlier, God implemented the 'tearing' process in many ways using economic and political problems to expose what lay hidden beneath the surface.

Today, when God tears, He may use some of the same tactics as He did when dealing with Northern Israel, or He may use other things to make His People aware a problem exists.

The following is a quick summary of some things that may indicate God is tearing, exposing problems to believers that they otherwise, simply do not see. This is not a complete list, by far, but it does give us give us an idea of what, God's tearing, might look like today.

SYMPTOM	REASON
Leadership proves faulty in one way or another	God hits leaders with a blow to scatter, break up and weaken their hold. God does this to take all eyes away from human leadership. This is good for both leaders and followers since the weakening of leadership causes many to return to God for answers and realignment. (In Hosea, this blow came to expose the false prophets and religious priests that taught the faith Jeroboam set up.)[16]
Beliefs seem lacking.	Unresolved problems stand out, as God proves things within the present belief system faulty or in need of realignment with His Word. That lack of resolve moves believers to seek YeHoVaH for answers. (Throughout the book of Hosea, one reads of God removing the corn and wine. This

---

[16] We mentioned this earlier in this study. Jeroboam built a faith parallel to the true faith but changed the priesthood and introduced idolatry. He kept the name of God as Yahweh, but added golden calf idols as representing the One who took them out of Egypt

	physical hunger was a tool of God, to prove their false faith inadequate. Hosea 2:8-9
Discontent and Unrest operative	Regarding the expression of their faith, people recognize emptiness within their present system of worship. Their unfulfilled desire for God propels them to seek Him. YeHoVaH shows them a way out of their discontent. (Hosea 2:13-22
People scatter	People, hurt for reasons too numerous to list, begin to wander away from the established system. Some find themselves in worse situations as prey for the wolves. Others seek YeHoVaH and find the needed answers.

If we perceive these and other similar things, as possible signs of the hand of God tearing, then, at the same time, as we press into God to resolve these, we will look for possible places where error, deception or unholy practices may exist and correct them. Once God's hand exposes the hidden problem, the worse thing we can do is to ignore it, blame others, or decide to keep things the way they are because we have always done things that way. It is far better to look at the purpose of God's tearing, identify what God's finger points out, then deal with it and move on with God.

REMEMBER: while God TEARS, He also HEALS
To explain the "healing", we will do a simple word comparison of the two Hebrew words: Torn and Heal.

HEWBREW WORD COMPARISON	
TORN טרף	**HEAL** רפה or רפא
Context within Hosea 6:1	
God intentionally surrounds (a person, nation, etc.)	
He exposes what is hidden	
He establishes His Headship	God establishes His Headship
He then scatters to break the whole and bring weakness	He sends His Word
The whole becomes fragmented or torn	His Word establishes and strengthens and makes whole (by His Spirit)

> **COMMENT:** God intentionally breaks or tears (due to stubborn disobedience and continual refusal to listen to Him). *The objective, once reached, causes those clinging to the "torn object" to release it, and then seek YeHoVaH, which brings a* return to Him, ending in a renewed relationship, correctly in alignment with truth. Healing follows.

BACK TO HOSEA:

Hosea further declared that God had smitten them and He would bind them up. What does the Hebrew picture word show us about these two words?

SMITTEN נכה	pronounced naw-kaw	**Strong's** **# 5221**
OVERALL WORD PICTURE MEANING:		
This word pictures indicates a blow deserved by actions, which cause one to surrender.		

COMMENTS: The word picture for "נ" (noon) suggests an inheritance. "כ" (kaf) shows a blow that comes as an inheritance. Simply put, actions receive their reward. The intentions of the action here is to discipline in order to bring about surrender so the person makes better choices. That 'blow' can be any tool YeHoVaH decides to implement, in order to help

His Child surrender to better life choice. It is a decision (or judgment) sent to correct.

Remember: The idea of correction shows the intentions of a good parent, correcting their child, meeting the circumstances, with the proper measure of discipline. Hebrews 12:6-7 makes it clear that, just as a human father corrects the waywardness of his child, God corrects His children. [17]

We need to keep in mind; *the aim of the correction is to bring believers into alignment with YeHoVaH and His Ways, resulting in* a fruitful life, which expresses the character of God, or simply put, is a life that looks like Yeshua".

Before leaving this section, let us be clear about discipline. We are not talking of something brutal, abusive or sadistic, but rather, the ability of a Sovereign, Loving God to reach into the life of His child, to introduce into that life, measures to turn them back to Him.

As human beings, we cannot possibly understand the depth or particular choice of those measures; however, when something touches our own life, perhaps events or things coming in rapid succession, we might take note to seek God, with an open mind, to discover *the*

---

[17] Hebrews 12:6-7

possibilities of things, in our life, that *God* considers offensive. If we have such, resolving the situation, with God's help, puts us back on track, and in the future, make better choices in things we embrace, or give access to, in our own life. [18] A return to YeHoVaH, removes the "smiting" and brings BINDING. What does that Hebrew Word picture, for binding, suggest?

BIND חבש	pronounced khaw-bash	Strong's # 2280
OVERALL WORD PICTURE MEANING:		
This word pictures indicates a protection like a wall or covering in order to separate the person from whatever afflicted them, like a bandage that protects a wound from further damage.		

Since the prophet Hosea used the word BIND in conjunction with the word, SMITTEN, how do these two words compare?

---

[18] Please note: This is not an indication that God sends disease, disaster, or other such things, **as measures to turn one back to God**. These measures will be such things as unanswered prayers, uncomfortable circumstances or incidents, etc. If disease or disaster does manifest, its root stems from the fallen state of the world, ha satan (the adversary) and other such things, but never from God.

HEBREW WORD COMPARISON	
SMITTEN naw-kaw'	**BIND** חבש khaw-bash'
Context of Hosea 6:1	
That inheritance (results of one's choices) brings correction.	A barrier to protect the individual or to wall out what wounds them
In this case, a discipline to cause one to surrender to receive the better ways of God.	In this case, wall out the discipline (as it is no longer necessary)
COMMENT: God smites because of one's choices in order to turn one back to Him. When God binds, He blocks the blow and walls out the object of wounding.	

In the verse immediately before our study of Hosea 6:1-3, we read:

Hosea 5: 15 I will go and return to my place, till they acknowledge their offence, and seek my face: in their affliction they will seek me early.

Here is a picture of God, under the First Covenant relationship, stepping back, *temporarily*, due to Northern Israel's sin. Then God allowed the adversary to do a work. In their affliction, God says, they (Northern Israel) will seek Him early. Afterwards, He then promises to bind them up, blocking out the blows, which caused the wounding.

RECAP OF HOSEA 6:1

Below is a wide paraphrase of the Hebrew words studied thus far in Hosea 6:1. Keep in mind, the intentions of this recap are not to replace the scripture interpretation in your bible. It is only a help to grasp the depth of the passage under study.

RECAP

A recap of the Hebrew Word pictures shows this:

> *The English text reads:* Come, and let us return unto YeHoVaH:
>
> *Hebrew Picture reads:* Draw near to God for a blessing from His Divine Power. Turn your backs on whatever things have kept you away from Him. Turn to the One Who promised to walk with you, doing wonders on your behalf making you victorious.
>
> *The English text reads* for he hath torn, and he will heal us; he hath smitten, and he will bind us up.

Hebrew Picture reads He surrounded us to expose the hidden things that caused us to stray and even though we may be scattered, He will make us whole again. He disciplines us because our choices were not right with Him, yet when we surrender, He will remove that which caused us such pain.

This paraphrase tells us much about our commitment to God, and God's commitment to us. Below is a chart recapping the Promises of God thus far studied.

\	REVIVAL'S PROMISE
Healing (from Hosea 6:1)	Having exposed what caused His people to stray, when they truly return, God makes them whole again
Binding (from Hosea 6:1)	Having corrected His People's disobedience, resulting from their wrong choices, once *they make better choices*, He *removes the pain* (the consequences) of their wandering

There are more promises within the latter part of the passage from Hosea 6:1-3, that indicate what happens once revival is underway. We will look at that later.

SECTION 2

IDENTIFYING REVIVAL

MARKING REVIVAL'S BEGINNINGS

2 Chronicles 5:1 to 7:4[19] speaks of a Revival in the beginning of the reign of King Solomon. Later we will use this Revival to indicate certain characteristics, from God's perspective, that apply to Revival. In this section, however, we will look at one important event in 2 Chronicles 5:1 to 7:4, to gain a handle on a key factor in recognizing Revival. In a latter section, we will look at that Revival in detail, defining Revival's characteristics.

POST TEMPLE DAYS
King David, a mighty King of Israel, amassed all the territory decreed to Israel. During his reign he brought the Ark of the Covenant, the symbol of God's Presence, into Jerusalem, the city of David, and situated it in a

---

[19] Before reading this chapter, please read 2 Chronicles 5:1 to 7:4.

special tent, where worshippers, singers and countless musicians ministered to YeHoVaH day and night.

Even though this reign of King David was impressive, expansive and powerful, YeHoVaH did not allow David to build a temple in which to place the Ark. Instead, God decreed that King David's son, Solomon, would have the honour of building God a temple. Yet King David did have a part to play, as during his reign, he stored up great treasures for this house of God.

King Solomon took the throne and in the fourth year of his reign, he began to build the temple, which took him seven years[20]. Solomon then chose a special feast day, the Feast of Tabernacles, for God's people to come to Jerusalem, rejoice in the celebration of the finished temple, and watch as the priests transported the Ark of the Covenant from the city of David to its honoured place within the temple.

THE ARK PLACED WITHIN THE TEMPLE
Since the Ark of the Covenant represented the presence of God, its entrance into the Temple was of marked importance. In 1 King 6, we read where YeHoVaH promised to dwell within that temple if certain conditions were met.

---

[20] 1 Kings 6:1; 1 Kings 6:38

| 1 Kings 6:11-14 | 11 ¶ And the word of YeHoVaH came to Solomon, saying, 12 Concerning this house which thou art in building, if thou wilt walk in my statutes, and execute my judgments, and keep all my commandments to walk in them; then will I perform my word with thee, which I spake unto David thy father: 13 And I will dwell among the children of Israel, and will not forsake my people Israel. 14 So Solomon built the house and finished it. |

The conditions are very clear:
- Walk in My statutes
- Execute My Judgments
- Keep all My Commandments to walk in them

God's Promises given:
- He will perform His Word to Solomon spoken to David, his father
- He will dwell among the children of Israel
- He will not forsake His people Israel

After this encounter, Solomon continued in the preparations to build the temple. Upon completion, the first order of business was to bring the Ark of the Covenant into the temple of YeHoVaH. The procedure to do so must follow biblical protocol, and so Solomon ensured all was in order. Then, adhering to every detail, God prescribed by Moses, to move the Ark, Solomon had the Ark placed within the temple.

While this was, a great occasion for both Solomon and the people, something significant happened here, which we must not overlook. The main purpose of the temple was to give the Ark *a place of rest.* Remember, the Ark of the Covenant was an important part of the belief system of Israel, since to them, it represented God's Presence in their midst. Moving the Ark into the Temple meant the Ark would have a "resting place".

> 1 Chronicles 28:2
>
> 2 "Then David the king stood up upon his feet, and said, Hear me, my brethren, and my people: [As for me], I [had] in mine heart ***to build an house of rest for the Ark of the cove***nant of YeHoVaH, and for the footstool of our God, and had made ready for the building:"

In summary, David saw the Ark of the Covenant brought to Jerusalem, but he could not put the 'Ark at rest' as that task, as God assigned it, belonged to his son, Solomon. Solomon completed the task as he built the temple. He assigned priests to carry the Ark into the Temple, after which, they removed the 'staves' (carrying poles) from the Ark[21]. From that point onward, the Ark rested within the established kingdom of Israel.

THE SIGNIFICANCE OF THE ARK AT REST[22]

A *Principle of Rest*, employed here, runs throughout the Bible from Genesis to Revelation, but believers rarely understand its purpose. In a concise recap, God finished His Works since the beginning of the world, and believers must rest in those finished works, including New Covenant believers.

> Hebrews 4:3 — 3 For we which have believed do enter into rest, as he said, As I have sworn in my wrath, if they shall enter into my rest: although the works were finished from the foundation of the world.

God's finished works are many, designed to touch every human life that ever breathed upon the earth, and for every life that believes in Him, God desires they enter His "rest".

---

[21] 2 Chronicles 5:9

[22] If you wish to know more about God's rest, consider two books by this same author. Consider "Thy Kingdom Come", Entering God's Rest in Prayer as it addresses the believer's rest. Or consider God's seventh prophetic day of rest studied in the book, "Heaven's Greater Government". Contact Cegullah Publishing for more information.

Not only was the purpose of the Temple to give the Ark rest, but the purpose of the Ark itself had to do with rest:

> Numbers 10:33-36
> 33 And they departed from the mount of YeHoVaH three days' journey: and the Ark of the covenant of YeHoVaH went before them in the three days' journey, *to search out a resting place for them*. 34 And the cloud of YeHoVaH [was] upon them by day, when they went out of the camp. 35 And it came to pass, when the Ark set forward, that Moses said, Rise up, YEHOVAH, and let thine enemies be scattered; and let them that hate thee flee before thee. 36 *And when it rested*, he said, Return, O YEHOVAH, unto the many thousands of Israel."

In short, when Israel went out daily, in the daylight, they followed the Ark. Symbolically, they walked in the pathway made for them by the Ark. When they declared, "Rise up, YEHOVAH, and let your enemies be scattered" they saw the Ark as the Presence of God going out before them and scattering or breaking the ranks of the enemy so they will have victory. When the Ark rested, that meant God returned from scattering the enemy.

That word **"return"** used in Numbers 10:36 is שׁוּב <# 7725>. Remember it means to turn away from what kept you in its grasp. Thus, the idea is this: *as the Ark went out, the enemy scattered; as the Ark returned, scattering ended for that day.* God went out before Israel then, and in this regard, Israel only need follow.

King David knew this principle as he declared it long before he took the throne of Israel.

| 1 Samuel 17:47 | 47 And all this assembly shall know that YeHoVaH saveth not with sword and spear: *for the battle is YeHoVaH'S,* and he will give you into our hands. |

At this time, David was but a boy when, under God's anointing, he went out to face a giant named Goliath. Even though a young boy, David knew the battle to take the Promised Land belonged to YeHoVaH and in this case, to dispossess the Philistines giant and all he defended. With confidence and faith, David faced the giant, removed his head and with his action of bravery, inspired all Israel to advance, to take the land God promised to them.

David's mindset was the same as the mindset given to the Israelites regarding the Ark going out before them. The Ark depicted God doing battle for Israel, making a clear path for His People to follow in victory. Unfortunately, not all the Israelites perceived the victory of Canaan Land in this manner. Instead, Israel saw the giants and the many chariots in the land and trembled in dread. They forgot that the battle belonged to YeHoVaH and thought it was in their hands alone. They did not rest in God's Victory but allowed fear, instead of faith, to compel them as the following scripture clearly states.

Hebrews 4:5-6	5 And in this place again, If they shall enter into my rest. 6 Seeing therefore it remaineth that some must enter therein, and they to whom it was first preached entered not in because of unbelief:

Due to their unbelief, the Israelites wandered for forty years in the desert. Unbelief robbed them of their rest. King David, on the other hand, was full of faith. He took all the territory promised to the Israelites and held it. This, however, meant constant war, but David, resting in God's promises, held the land.

In the promise that God made to King David, regarding Solomon, He said:

> 1 Chronicles 22:9
>
> 9 Behold, a son shall be born to thee, who shall be a man of rest; and I will give him rest from all his enemies round about: for his name shall be Solomon, and I will give peace and quietness unto Israel in his days.

In Solomon's days then, Israel, as well as the Ark had rest. The Ark remained within the Temple, never to go out to battle again and the nation was at peace. To keep that rest and peace intact, however, the people must remain faithful and loyal to YeHoVaH, obey His commands, or in short, ensure they put no idols before YeHoVaH.

Solomon failed to do that, and we see that by the end of Solomon's reign, he served other gods, and a great number of the people followed suit. Due to that idolatry, as you saw earlier, in the opening chapters of this book, God divided the nation in two. From then on, as the bible records, Israel, in bible days, never recovered from that division, the root of which was idolatry, although God did promise unity at some future date.

At this point, we will not focus on Israel's failure to enter their rest, but instead, remember the Ark at rest. That is a key factor regarding our topic, Revival.

GOD'S PRESENCE FILLS THE TEMPLE

In the next section, we will delve a little deeper into 1 Chronicles chapters 5 to 7, but at this point, we will look only at what is pertinent to the Ark at rest. In verse 7 to 9 of 1 Chronicles 5, we read:

> 1 Chronicles 5:7-9
>
> 7 And the priests brought in the Ark of the covenant of YeHoVaH unto his place, to the oracle of the house, into the most holy place, even under the wings of the cherubims: 8 For the cherubims spread forth their wings over the place of the Ark, and the cherubims covered the Ark and the staves thereof above. 9 *And they drew out the staves of the Ark*, that the ends of the staves were seen from the Ark before the oracle; but they were not seen without. And there it is unto this day.

Here we read the priests removed the staves, or poles they used to carry the Ark from place to place. This act of removing the staves clearly shows there is no longer a need to carry the Ark. This marked the beginning of the place of "Rest" for the Ark.

With the Ark in a place of rest, God did an exceptional thing. We read about that in the following passage:

> 2 Chronicles 5:13-14
>
> 13 It came even to pass, as the trumpeters and singers were as one, to make one sound to be heard in praising and thanking YeHoVaH; and when they lifted up their voice with the trumpets and cymbals and instruments of music, and praised YeHoVaH, saying, For he is good; for his mercy endureth for ever: *that then the house was filled with a cloud, even the house of YeHoVaH; 14 So that the priests could not stand to minister by reason of the cloud: for the glory of YeHoVaH had filled the house of God.*

Once the Ark rested, a cloud filled the house and the glory of YeHoVaH filled the house of God. In 2 Chronicles 6:1 we read that to Solomon, God kept His promise:[23]

---

[23] 1 Kings 6:13 "And I will dwell among the children of Israel, and will not forsake my people Israel."

| 2 Chronicles 6:1-2 | 1 ¶ Then said Solomon, YeHoVaH hath said that he would dwell in the thick darkness. 2 But I have built an house of habitation for thee, and a place for thy dwelling forever. |

As we will read in the next section, Solomon then speaks a powerful prophetic intercession on behalf of Israel, and then, YeHoVaH sends fire from heaven, which consumes the sacrifice on the altar, and for a second time on the same day, YeHoVaH fills that house with His glory. This first appearance of the glory however marks a significant thing: the beginning of the Revival.

REVIVAL'S BEGINNING

Many believers will look at the passage in 2 Chronicles and conclude that Revival begins at the point when the glory of YeHoVaH filled the house. The truth is, this phenomenon is God's indicator that something important happened, or some action prompted God to fill the house with His glory. That action, that important event, was the Ark in a state of rest. Therefore, while we see "the Glory of God filling the house" as an awesome and amazing sign, it is a result of another action, which pleased God: *"THE ARK AT REST"*.

Keep in mind, all previous activities prior to the Glory filling the temple, which we will specifically list in the next chapter, *are actually pre-revival activities, which bring the believer to the place of rest,* the point where *the believer ceases from their own works and begins to Rest in God's Work.* This gives God great pleasure, and thus, He fills His temple with His Glory.[24]

This thinking may require a paradigm shift for some readers; nevertheless, God's word directs believers to a place of rest, a place of faith, in order to please God, as the following scriptures declare:

Hebrews 4:1-3	1 ¶ Let us therefore fear, lest, a promise being left us of **entering into his rest**, any of you should seem to come short of it. 2 For unto us was the gospel preached, as well as unto them: but the word preached did not profit them, **not being mixed with faith** in them that heard it. 3 **For we which have believed do enter into rest**, as he said, As I have sworn in

---

[24] This is actually a prophetic picture of Salvation. The bulk of that teaching would make another chapter in itself, but to summarize it here, a believer 'rests' from their own works in order to be saved and then accepting Yeshua's works on the cross, they enter their rest. Then, the temple, their body, receives the Holy Spirit (as seen in the cloud and the glory filling the temple).

> my wrath, if they shall *enter into my rest*: although the works were finished from the foundation of the world.
>
> Hebrews 11:6 6 *But without faith it is impossible to please him: for he that cometh to God must believe that he is, and that he is a rewarder of them that diligently seek him.*

As we seek God to understand His Viewpoint on Revival, we must remember that a powerful aspect of *our faith* is that we first cease from our works, rest in God's finished works, and therefore, do things God's Way. That means we say goodbye to all the 'works of humankind which include things that "religion" brings with it. Instead, "rest" in what God alone ordained.

At this point, looking at the importance of the principle of Rest, we can conclude that the beginning of Solomon's revival came after the ark rested, at which point in time, the cloud came and the glory of YeHoVaH filled the house. This defines Revival's beginning from God's point of view:

Revival begins when believers enter *God's Rest*.

Following on with our habit of placing a chart summary at the end of specific factors for Revival, read the chart below.

REVIVAL'S BEGINNING	
Sign: The Ark at Rest (from 1 Chronicles 5:7-9)	Believers cease from their own works and enter God's Rest.

PRE-REVIVAL TRAITS

Having defined Revival's beginning, we can now detail some Pre-Revival characteristics looking at what happened before the Ark Rested. To make this simple, the first chart in this section outlines the actual physical preparations prior to the point that the Ark rested.

As you can see from the chart on the top of the next page, that many things took place prior to the special day when they brought the Ark of the Covenant from the city of David, to rest in the Temple. Originally, when King David brought the Ark into city of David it took two attempts. The first attempt failed simply because no one looked into the Word of God to understand how to handle the Ark but carried it their way, the result of which a man died[25].

---

[25] 2 Samuel 6:1-9

PREPARATIONS BEFORE THE ARK ENTERED THE TEMPLE
• Build and prepare the temple • Celebrated the Feast of Trumpets • Celebrated the Day of Atonement
PREPARATION AT TEMPLE COMPLETION
• Gathered the elders, tribe leaders • Gathered the priests • Gathered the people • Set the appointed day: The Feast of Tabernacles • Brought in the holy vessels • Carried in the Ark • Removed its staves (poles)

On the second attempt to bring up the Ark to the city of David, they carefully followed God's instructions, after which, the Ark, the king, the priests, the elders, and those that accompanied them on the journey to bring the Ark to Jerusalem, arrived safely.

As 2 Chronicles records, Solomon's move of the Ark from the city of David to the Temple, the priests were sanctified, bore the ark on their shoulders, and were accompanied by the elders of Israel, leaders of the tribes, and by a great accompaniment of singers, trumpeters, and musical instruments.

However, the preparations, before the time arrived to transfer the Ark, included the celebration of two important Feast Days, prior to the Feast of Tabernacles, the feast on which, Solomon chose to dedicate the temple and move the Ark. Those two feast days were the Feast of Trumpets and the Day of Atonement.

FEASTS PRIOR TO FEAST OF TABERNACLES

Below and on the next page are charts outlining the three (3) significant feasts celebrated around the time Solomon dedicated the temple.

All three feasts take place in the 7th month of the Hebrew calendar[26].

FEASTS IN THE 7TH MONTH		
Reference	Description	Prophetic Meaning
Leviticus 23:24	The 1st day of the 7th month which is a Sabbath (a Day of Rest) where the priests blew trumpets.	This feast prophetically announces YeHoVaH's coming.

---

[26] These feasts are in the fall of the year as they bring in the last yearly harvest.

Leviticus 16:29; Leviticus 23:27	On this one day (a Day of Rest) the people 'afflicted' their souls reflecting on their sins how they offended God. The High Priest on that day offered a Sin offering for all the people.	Yeshua's payment of our sins
Leviticus 23:34	Feast of Tabernacles, an 8day feast with 1st and 8th day as Days of Rest. The people built booths to dwell in to remind them of their sojourning in Israel.	Yeshua living in our midst. It is also a prophetic time, showing God's period of Rest for humankind.

Having established the events prior to the Ark Resting as descriptive of pre-Revival characteristics, here you will find a chart showing the name of the Feast with its particular characteristics of that feast and how it pertains to pre-Revival.

PRE-REVIVAL CHARACTERISTICS	
FEAST OF TRUMPETS	
Announcement of Trumpets that God is coming	Announcement by 'prophets' that He is coming[27].
A CALL TO RETURN TO YEHOVAH	A CALL TO RETURN TO YEHOVAH
• Be aware of His Coming	• Awareness of God's Coming (Messiah's Return)
• Get Ready	• Be Ready (Bride makes herself ready)[28]

DAY OF ATONEMENT	
PUT AWAY YOUR SINS	PUT AWAY YOUR SINS
• A call to reflect upon your sins	• A call to reflect upon your sins & ask forgiveness for them
• A call to receive God's sin provision • (covered by the blood of the animal)	• A call to receive God's provision for sin • (removed by the saving blood of Yeshua)
• Receive forgiveness	• Receive forgiveness

---

[27] Malachi 4:5 Behold, I will send you Elijah the prophet before the coming of the great and dreadful day of YeHoVaH: (John the Baptist, Spirit of Elijah)

[28] Revelation 19:7

Section 2 – Chapter 3 — Identifying Revival
Pre-Revival Traits

The Ark rested during the Feast of Tabernacles, so it is not pre-Revival. The list below, however, clearly sets out pre-revival characteristics.

PRE-REVIVAL CHARACTERISTICS RECAP	
1.	A clear call that God is coming (Yeshua is returning, and we must get ready. In *post bible Revivals*, we see this is also a common denominator. Each generation experiencing Revival had an awareness of the coming of Yeshua.
2.	A definite conviction of sin where there comes a turning away from sin to live as holy as the Bride makes herself ready for her Bridegroom[29]. This is also a common factor in post bible Revivals as well.

As you read this material, did you notice, God's call to His People includes a call to repent and to *"Return"* to Him? That call to repent and return to God often precedes an announcement of His Coming to the earth to bring judgment, but first in His Mercy, He extends

---

[29] John 16: 7 Nevertheless I tell you the truth; It is expedient for you that I go away: for if I go not away, the Comforter will not come unto you; but if I depart, I will send him unto you. 8 And when he is come, he will reprove the world of sin, and of righteousness, and of judgment: 9 Of sin, because they believe not on me; 10 Of righteousness, because I go to my Father, and ye see me no more; 11 Of judgment, because the prince of this world is judged.

an invitation to repent and return to Him. As that word 'return' # 7725 suggests, those who wish to return to Him, first must 'turn away from the things, whatever they might be, that keep them away from YeHoVaH". The return, then, happens in the pre-Revival stage.

Biblically speaking, repentance and returning are pre-Revival characteristics. *The return* to YeHoVaH characterises a response from true repentance, for if one is truly penitent, they desire to leave behind what has kept them from God, turning their backs on that thing. That shows true repentance.

RETURNING COMES BEFORE REVIVAL

Remember our introductory text from Hosea 6:

"1 Come, and let us return unto YeHoVaH: for he hath torn, and he will heal us; he hath smitten, and he will bind us up. 2 After two days will he revive us: in the third day he will raise us up, and we shall live in his sight. 3 Then shall we know, [if] we follow on to know YeHoVaH: his going forth is prepared as the morning; and he shall come unto us as the rain, as the latter [and] former rain unto the earth."

Verse 1 shows the same Pre-Revival Characteristics as shown in 2 Chronicles. It begins with the invitation to come. Remember this word promises a drawing close to give a blessing. Next is the call to Return, a serious action on the part of the believer whereby the person forsakes their sin leaving it behind for the things of God.

This chart summarizes these thoughts.

COMPARISON PRE-REVIVAL CHARACTERISTICS # 1	
Hosea 6:1	2 Chronicles 5
COME:	HE IS COMING (Seen in the Feast of Trumpets as an Awareness of the Coming of YeHoVaH) [announced by trumpets]
RETURN:	PUT AWAY YOUR SINS (Seen in the Day of Atonement, when one reflects upon their sins and seeks God for His forgiveness, as the person turns away from whatever kept them from God.) [Put away your sins and receive God's forgiveness]

The next chart adds one more column to this: the way it is in the Apostolic Scriptures. Before going there, listen to Peter in the book of Acts who verifies the pattern:

Foundations of Revival   Biblical Evidence of Revival

Acts 3:19   19 Repent ye therefore, and be converted, that your sins may be blotted out, when the times of refreshing shall come from the presence of YeHoVaH;

Repent, as the Greek Word indicates, means one makes a decision and changes their mind. The Word 'converted' indicates a complete turnaround from present behaviour. "That your sins may be blotted out" states forgiveness. Peter then extends a promise of 'refreshing'. This word indicates a cool breeze suggestive of the Holy Spirit.

This refreshing is also seen in the two texts we studied: 2 Chronicles: After the Feast of Trumpets and Day of Atonement comes the Feast of Tabernacles representing the Presence of God dwelling with humankind. Hosea 6:2 promises God will 'revive'. As explained earlier, this word, in a truly spiritual sense, means being full of God's Breath, for this is *life*. Further on into verse 3 of Hosea 6, we see a promise of refreshing which we will look at in further detail later.

Put all these three scriptures together and we have a good indicator of pre-Revival characteristics that are biblical and know we can expect today! The following chart summaries these pre-Revival characteristics for us:

Section 2 – Chapter 3   Identifying Revival
Pre-Revival Traits

COMPARISON PRE-REVIVAL CHARACTERISTICS # 2			
Hosea 6:1	2 Chronicles 5	Acts 3: 19	Today
COME:	HE IS COMING	HE HAS COME	HE IS COMING AGAIN
RETURN:	PUT AWAY YOUR SINS	PUT AWAY YOUR SINS Repent Return (Be converted)	PUT YOUR SINS AWAY (Return)
Hosea 6:2-3 REVIVED	REVIVED (seen in Feast of Tabernacles)	BE REFRESHED	BE REFRESHED

In every scripture reference, YeHoVaH extended the invitation, *waiting for His People to respond*. Perhaps we overlook this important fact, the fact that *we have an important part to play*.

When we study the scriptures and see that *our part happens in the pre-Revival stages, we must begin to look at our own life and with the help of the Holy Spirit, see if we have strayed in any way*. If so, we return to Him! We repent from ways in which we offended Him, and then receive forgiveness, forsaking those things and moving on from there. God does promise that returning to Him with all our hearts, mind, soul and strength produces results.

In the remainder of this book, we will continue to see Revival from God's perspective, but for now, remember, God's perspective for *pre-Revival* is this: God gives the call

1. You respond
2. You return
3. You forsake (your sins whatever offended Him)

> **Recognize where biblical revivals begin.**
> **Do your part & God will do His!**

Continuing with our pattern to recap the main theme at the sections end, read the chart on the next page.

PRE-REVIVAL CHARACTERISTICS SUMMARIZED	
(using 2 Chronicles 5)	
Feast of Trumpets	• Call to Return • Announcement that He is coming
Day of Atonement	• Repent of your sins • Receive Forgiveness • Forsake whatsoever caused you to stray

PERSONAL REFLECTION

Most believers do not wish to offend God, however inadvertently it happens. The fact is that, although we try, we do not always do things God's Way, but more often, we do what is right *in our own eyes*. Take some time and ask God to open the eyes of your understanding to see if you truly understand and walk in His Ways.

EARLY REVIVAL TRAITS

2 Chronicles 5:1 to 2 Chronicles 7:4 relates the Revival in the reign of Solomon. From that passage on Revival, we have one clear dividing line between *pre-Revival and Revival*, and a second dividing line, which separated **the early characteristics of Revival** from *a full-fledged Revival*.

Everything *prior* to the cloud descending upon the Temple and the Glory of YeHoVaH filling the Temple, shows **pre-Revival**. From the 1st filling of the House with God's glory to the second incidence of the same, reveals early beginnings of Revival. Everything from when the fire from heaven fell and consumed the sacrifice, onward, indicates full-fledged Revival.[30]

To make that simple, here it is in chart form.

---

[30] Provided the believer desires to live his or her life as a living sacrifice. If not, the revival will wane

REVIVAL STAGES		
PRE- REVIVAL	*2 Chronicles 5:1 to 14*	(sanctify priests, move Ark to place of rest)
REVIVAL	*2 Chronicles 6:1 to 7:1*	(after ark rested, cloud came & then Solomon's prophetic Intercession)
FULLFLEDGED REVIVAL	*2 Chronicles 7:1 -9*	Fire consumes the sacrifice

INTERCESSION & COMPASSION FOR OTHERS

The prayer in 2 Chronicles 6 begins as Solomon gives thanks to YeHoVaH for His goodness and faithfulness in fulfilling His Word. Then the prayer changes tone, as Solomon prays a prayer of repentance for the present and future people of Israel. His compassionate and moving prayer petitions YeHoVaH to forgive and restore His people.

Most likely, Solomon planned his prayer earlier, since he made a large scaffold on which to speak with God and the people. However, Solomon did not release that prayer until after the ark rested within the Temple, and the cloud descended and filled the Temple with glory. This would strongly suggest that Solomon could not pray that intercession on his own, but rather, needed the power of God in which to utter it, especially considering its prophetic content.

In the action of the fire from heaven, in the First Covenant Revival, we see the pleasure and power of God applied to the waiting sacrifice. In this, we see, even in our New Covenant faith, God's desire to consume the believer in every aspect of their being. That being the case, the believer willingly dies for their Lord, and lives so sold out to Him, that nothing shakes them from their course to follow YeHoVaH. These indicate the best results of repenting, returning and relying upon God for new beginnings.

DOWNFALL OF SOLOMON'S REVIVAL
Solomon's Revival started well but did not finish well. Many reasons made up the Revival's sad end, the primary reason being 'self' got in the way as Solomon worshipped idols.

Thus, within this Revival, we can see its downfall. Rather than going into detail, we have included a simple chart for your review.

DOWNFALL OF REVIVAL
COMPROMISE Solomon made an alliance with Pharaoh when he married the Pharaoh's daughter. This speaks of *compromise with the world*. 1 Kings 3:1
PROPSPERITY'S SNARE Solomon prospered exceedingly and he set his sights to enjoy all he had, without restraint, even overtaxing the people to sustain his lifestyle. Earlier, the riches collected went to adorn the temple, but Solomon spent 13 years building elaborate houses where he and his seven hundred wives, princesses and three hundred concubines lived. 1 Kings 7:1; 1 Kings 11:4b to 6
IDOLATRY The Word of YeHoVaH makes it clear that "when Solomon was old, that his wives turned away his heart after other gods: and his heart was not perfect with YeHoVaH his God, as was the heart of David his father. For Solomon went after Ashtoreth the goddess of the Zidonians, and after Milcom the abomination of the Ammonites. And Solomon did evil in the sight of YeHoVaH, and went not fully after YeHoVaH, as did David his father." 1 Kings 11:4b to 6

UNHEEDED WARNINGS
Solomon did not see the continuation of his son on the throne of all Israel for YeHoVaH divided the nation under his son, Rehoboam (read 1 Kings 9:1-9).

FORSOOK YEHOVAH[31]
Solomon turned away from YeHoVaH and in doing so invited the people to do the same. 1 King 9:6-9 says " Because they forsook YeHoVaH their God, who brought forth their fathers out of the land of Egypt, and have taken hold upon other gods, and have worshipped them, and served them: therefore hath YeHoVaH brought upon them all this evil."

What a sad end for Solomon who began so well. That latter end stands out as a warning to all, for Solomon's life, with no restraints, fed a problem within his heart. While Solomon oversaw the sacrifice of many offerings to God, he never gave his life as a pleasing sacrifice to YeHoVaH. Instead, he did whatever was 'right' in his own eyes'; no matter the many warnings that he received even from God, Himself. Revival's continuation is not about repeated appearances of supernatural phenomena. It is not about the glory and

---

[31] A study of Solomon's life and his idolatry which carried on into the lives of his sons in Judah, opened a door to a marriage with Jezebel's daughter, Athaliah. A hidden enemy of Revival is the Spirit of Jezebel.

pomp of religious ceremonies or adornments for a building. It is not about creating an influence to draw great crowds of people at the cost of losing oneself to sin. Revival is about allowing the fires of God to purge, cleanse, and change one. It is about keeping the believer, the 'sacrifice' on the altar. It must be as the Apostle Paul said: "I beseech you therefore, brethren, by the mercies of God, that ye present your bodies a living sacrifice, holy, acceptable unto God, which is your reasonable service." [32]

To recap the early traits of Revival in this chapter, read the chart below.

EARLY REVIVAL TRAITS (from 2 Chronicles 5)	
Intercession	Revival leads one to a place of deep intercession, where one intercedes for others, within and without the church, and takes one to that place of total dedication to God.
Consumed by God	The fire of God falls, as one becomes a living sacrifice on God's altar, making one willing to give all unto YeHoVaH.

---

[32] Romans 12:1

FULL-FLEDGED REVIVAL TRAITS

In the last section, we described Solomon's Revival where fire fell from heaven and consumed the sacrifice. At that point, we saw full-fledged Revival and compared it with New Covenant thinking, however, that description did not describe some of the benefits arising from Revival. In order to see those benefits in detail, we will look at the remaining portions of the scripture, with which we opened this book.

*Come, and let us return unto YeHoVaH: for he hath torn, and he will heal us; he hath smitten, and he will bind us up. After two days will he revive us: in the third day he will **raise** us up, and we shall **live** in his **sight**. Then shall we **know**, if we **follow on** to know YeHoVaH: his **going forth*** is prepared as the morning; and he shall **come** unto us as the **rain**, as the latter and former rain unto the earth.[33]

Hosea 6:1-3

First, let us refresh our memory and recap our teachings so far regarding this verse.

English reads:	*Come, and let us return unto YeHoVaH: for he hath torn, and he will heal us; he hath smitten, and he will bind us up.*
Hebrew Picture reads:	*Draw near to God for a blessing from His Divine Power. Turn your backs on whatever things have kept you away from Him. Turn to the One Who promised to walk with you, doing wonders on your behalf making you victorious. He surrounded us to expose the hidden things that caused us to stray and even though we may be scattered, He will make us whole again. He disciplines us because our choices were not right with Him, yet when we surrender; He will remove that which caused us such pain.*

---

[33] Please note that PROMISED REVIVAL never came to Northern Israel in the time of Hosea.

While we looked at the word, "revive", we did not recap it within the verse setting. Here it is now in its setting.

| English reads: | After two days he will revive us ... |

| Hebrew Picture reads: | After two days (referring to the time of breaking then finished), He will wall out every work that removes His breath, or that does not produce His Life. (Remember this carries a picture of full of His Life) |

This word "revive" shows us the beginning of the Revival and from the words, "he will raise us up" and onwards show the many characteristics of a full-fledged Revival. Thus, in this section, we will look at the remaining highlighted (bolded) words in this passage.

REMAINING WORDS IN HOSEA 6:1-3
"HE WILL RAISE US UP"

RAISE קום	Pronounced koom	Strong's # 6965
OVERALL WORD PICTURE MEANING:		
This word picture indicates a lifting above to establish one as powerful. KJV interpreted this word in other places as "established or powerful".		

Some powerful imagery stands out in this word, for example, the letter מ (mem) shows a picture of mighty waters. By the use of the letter ק (qof) we see that the origin of the established power came from above, beyond humankind. It is clear from the Hebrew Word picture then, that this 'raising' cannot be done by the hand of humankind and when it happens, it brings a powerful burst of life with it.

Obviously, if in the word 'revive' we see an exclusion to the anything not from God's breath or Spirit, that imagery carries over to God alone doing the work, by His Mighty Holy Spirit. Regarding, "raising up", the imagery includes a mighty elevation, *above* what formerly oppressed, crushed or broke a people. The former "tearing' and the earlier period of 'smiting' has finished, and the 'healing and binding' has begun.

"AND WE SHALL LIVE"
In an earlier section, we looked at the word "LIFE", rooted from the same word as revive. The revived people arise to a place of life, true life, as God sees it and desires it, for humankind. Remember, in the word picture for life, every work that stopped God's Spirit from expressing His works ceased. Thus, we have a people raised above what crushed them and they receive life.

"IN HIS SIGHT"

SIGHT פנים	pronounced paw-neem	Strong's # 6440
OVERALL WORD PICTURE MEANING:		
This word pictures suggests a person positioned in such a manner as to turn towards someone (or something) in order to receive from them a mighty work. It means "in the face of".		

This is a good picture to show the continuation of the revived state.

"THEN SHALL WE KNOW"

ידע KNOW	Pronounced yaw-dah	Strong's # 3045
OVERALL WORD PICTURE MEANING:		
The word picture shows a work or deed entering through a doorway, in an eye-to-eye agreement. The bible uses this to explain the mutual, consenting, agreement to a sexual union, between husband and wife. It indicates their intimate relationship. It is to "know" by experience; to totally reveal oneself.		

"Then shall we know", indicates a continuation in the close relationship with YeHoVaH, expressed in the earlier parts of the verse, where He revives and raises up. It shows an agreement which with God, in the way He sees and does things.

"IF WE FOLLOW ON TO KNOW³⁴ YEHOVAH"

FOLLOW ON רדף	pronounced raw-daf	Strong's # 7291
OVERALL WORD PICTURE MEANING:		
This word pictures indicates a sole focus or 'leadership' to pursue a thing, to follow after it.		

Someone who "follows on" is someone who pursues relentlessly, without ceasing. Keeping it within its verse context, compiling this thought with the subject 'to know', you have a beautiful picture of a person pursuing a close, intimate connection with YeHoVaH, the One in Whom they find their total satisfaction.

"HIS GOING FORTH"
(Chart on next page)

GOING FORTH מוצא	pronounced mowtsa	Strong's # 4161

---

[34] This is the same Hebrew word for "know" as in the first part of that verse # 3045 in Strong's Exhaustive Concordance

> **OVERALL WORD PICTURE MEANING:**
>
> This word pictures indicates a source like a spring of water that moves one along on a powerful journey. Something flows, out of a source, like water. KJV has interpreted it twice as water springs.

Thus, as God 'goes forth', He "bursts forth". The word picture shows Him as full of water, full of the things that satisfy the thirst. It is a powerful, bursting forward, suggesting waters accompanying Him. This fits well with the imagery of the 'rain'!

"IS PREPARED AS THE MORNING"

The meaning here suggests that it is set in place, like the morning. In other words, the time of His coming is as sure as the morning.

"HE SHALL COME UNTO US AS THE RAIN"

We looked at the word "come" earlier as indicting a drawing near to God, drawing close for the sole purpose of attachment to that person. In this case, YeHoVaH shall come as the rain. The word rain has interesting imagery, too.

Full-Fledged Revival

RAIN גשם	pronounced gheh' shem	Strong's # 1653
OVERALL ORIGINAL WORD PICTURE MEANING:		
This word pictures indicates water pouring (coming) forth		

THE PICTURE OF GOD SHOWN HERE IS THAT HE IS LIKE WATER, THE SOURCE & SUSTAINER OR LIFE

LATTER & FORMER RAIN UNTO THE EARTH

This refers to the seasons of rain, former meaning the early harvest in the spring, in which it waters that planting, and latter meaning watering the crops for the harvest reaped in the fall.

PUTTING IT ALL TOGETHER

The English text reads: *After two days will he revive us: in the third day, he will **raise** us up, and we shall **live** in his **sight**.*

Hebrew Picture reads: *After two days (referring to the time of breaking now finished), He will wall out every work that removes His breath, or that does not produce His Life. He will powerfully lift us up above all that formerly*

	oppressed us, so we will walk above it. We will have true life (nothing to hinder His Spirit bringing life to us) for His Face is towards us and ours is towards Him.
The English text reads:	*Then shall we **know**, if we **follow on** to know YeHoVaH: his **going forth** is prepared as the morning; and he shall **come** unto us as the **rain**, as the latter and former rain unto the earth*
Hebrew Picture reads:	*With all that in place, we will share a close an intimate knowledge of Him and be in agreement with Him. (There is a picture here of a covenant relationship as in marriage.) If we pursue this aspect to know Him and continue to agree with Him, His approach to us will be as sure as the morning and will bring a powerful burst of refreshing water like the rain that comes to bring forth the harvests, spring and fall.*

Once again, this amplified presentation is not a replacement for the written text in the King James Version of the bible or other versions. This simply shows us the qualities of a relationship with God after He revives us. Some of those characteristics are:
- A blessing from God
- A release of all things not sourced in Him
- A walling out of what is not from Him
  - A powerful elevation above our circumstances

- A focus on God to love and serve Him
- A continual agreement with the Ways of God
- An intimate connection with Him (covenant agreement)
- A steady, unwavering pursuit of that relationship
- A promised bursting forth of His Spirit to quench our thirst
- A promised life with great fruitfulness, a great harvest

A FULL-FLEDGED REVIVAL

The characteristics above speak of the quality of a full-fledged Revival. The water, as always, speaks of His Holy Spirit, of which there is an overabundance of His Presence. As for the believer, there is a constant, continual pursuit of the relationship with God, seeking not the external good things from the relationship but the satisfying relationship coming from a connection with the Person of God, discovered in the relationship. Such a pursuit results in a powerful journey, producing a great harvest, both in the life of the person revived and in the lives of others.

This truly revived state, with its flowing rivers of refreshing waters, is more than speaking in a language not learned that we call tongues[35]. This goes beyond

---

[35] John 7:38

that initial experience of a first encounter with God, but is an incessant pursuit of the relationship with God, to operate in oneness with Him.

This relationship is like two people, locked into a marriage, where each partner desires the other partner to soar, to their mutual satisfaction of their life together. The literal picture shows two lives flowing together with the waters from above, from God, mingling with the waters of the one from the earth, with the believer. The two waters, thus intermingled, will lose their separateness and flow as one. Onlookers cannot tell one from the other. That, however, does not mean a loss of individual identity, but rather a fulfillment from within, which results in a flow of oneness, to one cause, for one purposes. In other words, they share the same goals.

Speaking of the believer's life in God, there flows a unity with God and from that oneness, comes the development and release of the divine nature of God. This is a true *picture of Revival*! To quote the Apostle Peter:

| 1 Peter 5:1-8 | 1 ¶ Simon Peter, a servant and an apostle of Jesus Christ, to them that have obtained like precious faith with us through the righteousness of God and our Saviour Jesus Christ: 2 Grace and peace be multiplied unto |

you through the knowledge of God, and of Jesus our Lord, 3 According as his divine power hath given unto us all things that pertain unto life and godliness, through the knowledge of him that hath called us to glory and virtue:

4 Whereby are given unto us exceeding great and precious promises: that by these ye might be partakers of the divine nature, having escaped the corruption that is in the world through lust.

5 And beside this, giving all diligence, add to your faith virtue; and to virtue knowledge; 6 And to knowledge temperance; and to temperance patience; and to patience godliness; 7 And to godliness brotherly kindness; and to brotherly kindness charity. 8 For if these things be in you, and abound, they make you that ye shall neither be barren nor unfruitful in the knowledge of our Lord Jesus Christ.

In closing the description of biblical Revival, to see the REVIVED PERSON is to see the ONE FROM ABOVE.

In other words, the believer looks like their God! This image happens as the believer develops a continual agreement with their covenant partner, YeHoVaH, as they bow their knee to His Ways, recognizing they are best.

Revived believers, walking hand in hand with God, accept and allow the continual development of His Ways, thus allowing a removal of anything that takes them away from expressing the overall picture of God's Character and Divine Nature. It goes past the individual entity, to the corporate entity of Bride of Messiah. Onlookers see only Yeshua, moving and breathing in their midst.

Reading the book of Acts, we see this expression of Yeshua as a reality, as the early Christian church advanced forward from the initial launch at Pentecost. The First Covenant never had the privilege to partake of God's Divine Nature, as we do. Only in the New Covenant, after Yeshua paid the price, attained the victory, and fulfilled His Purpose upon the earth, and then sent the Holy Spirit to live in our human temple, is such a thing ever heard of!

FULL-FLEDGED REVIVAL TRAITS (Hosea 6:1-3 passage)	
Revived, Raised up, Follow on to Know YeHoVaH, His going forth prepared, former, and latter rain	• A promised bursting forth of His Spirit, and a release and walling out of all things not sourced in Him • An intimate connection with God, in a steady, unwavering pursuit of a relationship that places Him first, thus, loving and serving Him above all • others, and above all things • A full agreement with God's Ways, with unwavering • obedience to them • A change, by His Spirit, whereby we flow with His Divine Nature • An elevation, by God's Spirit, to walk above all circumstances bringing in God's will and giving Him glory • A life filled with fruitfulness, and a great harvest in the things of God, for God[36].

---

[36] There are more characteristics, but these are the ones shown in this segment of the book using the scripture passage found in Hosea 6:1-3

SECTION 3

NEW COVENANT REVIVAL 4

All the evidence, thus far in this book, points to a *First Covenant* style Revival. We have yet to look at New Covenant Revival. To do that, let us begin with a question:

If the New Covenant exceeds the First Covenant in greatness, (and it does) how would that affect Revival?

One might answer this question by saying, "it would be far greater, far better" than the First Covenant, and that Apostolic authors would bring out that 'greatness' in their writings. Unfortunately, to the disappointment of many, the Apostolic scriptures simply do not directly speak of Revival. The closest mention of the subject is in the book of Acts, where the apostle, Peter, said:

Acts 3:   *19 Repent ye therefore, and be converted, that your sins may be blotted out, when the times of refreshing shall come from the presence of YeHoVaH;*

We know the target audience receiving this message were Jews and some proselytes of Judaism who came to Jerusalem to celebrate the feasts of Passover and Shavuot[37]. The body of Peter's message invited them to recognize Yeshua as the fulfillment of the scriptures and thus realizing He was the Messiah, make a decision, to repent and follow Him from then on. In their acceptance of Yeshua, Peter promised God would blot out their sins, and then each one would receive a "refreshing", which, in its context, indicated a breeze or wind, in reference to the Holy Spirit.

This message from Peter did not apply to believers gathered in the Upper Room but rather to the listening audience of Jews and proselytes. Furthermore, as one reads the entire New Covenant, there is not one passage found informing New /Renewed Covenant believers of a need for Revival. Even in the book of Revelation where Yeshua speaks to those seven churches that wandered away from their early beginnings, there is not one shred of evidence where

---

[37] Christians call this feast Pentecost.

He tells them that they should consider Revival as a solution.

Yeshua's basic message, to those churches, is a call to REPENT, or as the Greek word implies, go in another direction, or change their present course of service to Him. Yeshua promised those churches rewards for overcoming their wandering, but again, He never mentioned Revival. His Message, to one church that disappointed Him, included a promise that He would blow out their candlestick, since they had lost their first love. Yet, He neither mentioned Revival, as an option, nor gave a promise to relight their candlestick.

If Revival had been the viable answer to any one of the seven churches addressed in the Book of Revelation, which many think represent the Ekklesia throughout the ages, surely the dialogue within the book of Revelation would mention a call to Revival. Yet no call exists, not in the seven messages to those seven churches and not even within the Apostolic Writings within the entire New Covenant.

WHY IS THE WORD REVIVAL NOT MENTIONED IN THE NEW COVENANT?

There are some theories as to why New Covenant authors never spoke of Revival. Some conjecture that the Apostolic Writings came to a church already living in Revival, merely struggling with the basic steps of living out their new faith. Their faith, while similar to the First Covenant, was radically different and they were not sure of the dynamics of the Holy Spirit dwelling w1`ithin them. They were not in need of an awakening, or revival, but rather of clarity on how to live within the New Covenant setting.

Supporters of that point of view state that God, in His Sovereignty and Foreknowledge, did not find it necessary to speak of Revival since that church lived in Revival, as should every New Covenant Christian. These conclude that, if it been necessary for further generations of Christians to seek God for Revival, the Apostles, led by the Spirit, would surely have recorded it, but no such passage exists.

There are other theories too but exploring those theories, as all theories, only gives us, after all, a theory. We need solid biblical evidence in which to base our faith. We must look past theories, then, to look at the truth, or the bottom line within the Apostolic Scriptures regarding the topic of Revival. First, however, let us take a quick summary of Church History for, in that, we see a need for Revival, and the actions of the Holy Spirit, to correct the problem.

To examine church history in detail is a long and intricate study and at best, here, we could only summarize it. An overview of the subject, however, shows us that by looking back at the problem, as well as the solution, implemented by the Holy Spirit, that there is an interesting pattern. First, the Church veered away from its original foundation and embraced what God did not desire for them and so they needed to "return" to God. Secondly, in their "returning", in every case, there was one common denominator:

God restored a buried and forgotten truth that the early church knew and expressed.

Looking back, not so much on the problem then, but rather on the solution God implemented, we can easily identify that the church shifted away from her moorings. In addition, we can see that truth, once buried, became exposed and restored, and thus realigned the church, bit by bit, with God's requirements for New Covenant living. Interestingly enough too, as the Holy Spirit restored each buried truth, we also see an important pattern or blueprint which God followed for the restoration of the church. That important pattern matches closely to God's blueprint of a First Covenant "shadow" or "type":

The Tabernacle of Moses.

As we look at God's Plan of Restoration, keep in mind God placed these "shadows or types" within the First Covenant, but these find their understanding in light of the Apostolic Scriptures. When looking at the First Covenant shadow of the Tabernacle of Moses, since that is the pattern God seems to have followed, it helps us to understand God's direction for the church today, including His plan for restoration wherever the church, wandered from its roots.

SHADOW OF RESTORATION IN THE FIRST COVENANT

Under the First Covenant, the Tabernacle of Moses showed a *progressive way* into the Presence of God, accessed only by God's chosen order of priests, called Levites. Beginning at the gate or entrance point and moving towards the Holy of Holies, we find a brazen altar standing ready to receive acceptable offerings for God.

Next, after the acceptable offering, the priest stopped at the 'laver' or a place of washing. With clean hands and feet, the priest moved forward on his journey to the place of God's Presence, by entering the first part of the tent or tabernacle known as the Holy Place. As he entered the Holy Place, he walked past five tall pillars positioned at the entrance, as a support for the roof covering.

Standing then, within the Holy Place, the priest came to a large, seven-branched Menorah or Candlestick, which shed its light on the other two articles of furniture within the Holy Place. These articles included an altar of incense where the priest made additional offerings to God, and a table of showbread that held 12 loaves of bread, one for every tribe of Israel.

Moving closer to the Place of God's Presence, there stood four large pillars supporting a heavy veil, which separated the Holy Place from the Holy of Holies. These acted as a barrier, which said "Stop", to every priest except one, the High Priest. He could only enter the Holy of Holies once a year and, he must have with him, in a basin, the blood of the sacrificial offering. Taking the basin with the blood with him, the priest, cautiously and prayerfully pulled back the curtain and entered the Holy of Holies.

Once in the Holy of Holies, the only article of furniture there, the Ark of the Covenant, which represented God's Presence, stood stately and regally before the priest. This Ark, a chest like box made of pure gold, held within, the commandments of God, a pot of manna from Israel's days of wandering in the desert and a rod of Aaron, which signified God's choice of priesthood. On the top of the golden chest, there sat a Mercy Seat, also made of pure gold. It was upon that Mercy Seat, that the High Priest sprinkled the sacrificial blood.[38] Moving carefully and reverently

---

[38] There are many good studies available on this topic. If you, dear reader, are not familiar with that study, you might explore the possibilities of taking a course on it.

out of that hallowed place, the High Priest left the Presence of God.

Looking back now on Church History, and using this Tabernacle of Moses as a blueprint, we can see how God restored the wandering church. Each article of furniture, within the Tabernacle of Moses depicts a once buried truth that God restored. As you explore the details of this blueprint on the following pages, please remember that believers in the New Covenant do not access God in stages, such as under the First Covenant.

Also, remember our consideration on this blueprint, merely **indicates the necessary steps** that God took **to restore truth** to the church. Thus, it could reach its goal: *returning to operate as the early church, which looked, in character and action, exactly like Yeshua, of whom the Tabernacle of Moses foreshadowed.*

The chart in this section, entitled "God's Plans of Restoration for the Ekklesia", shows, in the first column, the articles of furniture with the Tabernacle of Moses.

It follows a progression, beginning at the outer court where you find:
- the Brazen Altar
- the Laver, where the progression continues into the Holy Place, where you find:
- the first Veil with its 5 pillars
- the Holy Place including the:
  - Candlestick
  - Altar of Incense
  - Table of Shewbread
  - the Second Veil with its 4 pillars

Lastly, that column shows:
- the Holy of Holies, with the Ark of the Covenant, upon which, sat the Mercy Seat

The second column shows what practices occupied the Ekklesia at that time, which buried the truth.

The last column shows the most common name for each post-bible Revival, as well as the main activity of that Revival, which indicates the restored truth.

GOD'S PLANS OF RESTORATION FOR THE EKKLESIA			
BEGINNING AT THE OUTER COURT			
FURNITURE	BURIED TRUTH		RESTORED TRUTH
The brazen altar: • The place of Repentance • The place of Sacrifice for sin	**CHURCH PRACTICES:** • Earn your salvation through works • Good works outweigh bad= heaven • The Church is the Ultimate Authority		**PROTESTANT REFORMATION** • Salvation by faith alone • Yeshua's blood only acceptable offering • The Word of God is the Ultimate Authority
The laver: • The place for cleansing • The place for sanctification	**CHURCH PRACTICES:** • Living according to church law to be sanctified • Outward expressions of holiness, e.g. dress, postures for prayer, etc.		**HOLINESS MOVEMENT:** • Cleansed by Yeshua's blood • Sanctified through the Word • Inward expressions of holiness: e.g. restoration of the fruit of the Spirit

The order listed here does not suggest the order in which the restoration appeared.

MOVING INTO THE HOLY PLACE:		
(It seems as if YeHoVaH pulled back the roof, the covering and exposed the inside)		
The 5 Pillars (which held first veil)	CHURCH PRACTICES: • Strong leaders rule • Church practices define those who can minister within any given church body	APOSTOLIC MOVEMENT • 5-fold offices of the church restored • Individual gifting of believers recognized
The Candlestick • The place for light within the House	CHURCH PRACTICES: • Sickness, disease, forms of suffering, etc. part of the regular faith life • Gifts of the Spirit not possible (seen as passed away)	PENTECOSTAL MOVEMENT • Healing part of the atonement & available for all believers • Restoration of the gifts of the Spirit
The Table of Shewbread • The place of Fellowship with God and with brethren	CHURCH PRACTICES: • Denominational lines drawn and kept • Nation of Israel not necessary or important	CHARISMATIC OUTPOURING • Pull down denominational lines • The nation of Israel important to God and to the church

	CONTINUING IN THE HOLY PLACE	
The Altar of Incense • The place of prayer, praise and worship	CHURCH PRACTICES: • Rote prayers • Ritualistic worship	PRAYER MOVEMENT • Holy Spirit inspired prayers • Holy Spirit inspired worship a lifestyle flowing from Holy Spirit driven prayer and worship
HOLY OF HOLIES		
4 pillars & veil • Yeshua's body torn for us	CHURCH PRACTICES: • Operate from tradition of leadership and ritual practices • Church traditions replaced Feasts of YeHoVaH • Humanistic teachings • Teachings of the world	HEBRAIC MOVEMENT • Return to the roots of the scriptural faith • Revelation, exposure and removal of all Babylonian, Hellenistic, Humanistic, Traditional, Rabbinical and other practices *contrary to scripture*

The cherubim are 4 in number and according to the Word, guard the holiness of God. If man is to enter through the 'veil' they must do so through Yeshua's blood and operate from that place of 'holiness' given at the cross. This revival will place man operative in true holiness without the practices of the world.

This brings us up to date with where we are now. The next move of God should expose whatever believers have embrace to stop their ability to rest and move within the Presence of God. This move should be one of the intensified fires of the Holy Spirit, as the Bride makes herself ready for Her Groom! It will include a powerful, heart-felt measure of worship, as in the days of King David, during the time of the Tabernacle of David. It should reap an end time harvest!

The Ark, cloud and Glory of God	CHURCH PRACTICES: Yet to be exposed	NO NAME YET GIVEN
		Details not yet known but a summary would say "moving in power, in complete New Testament power, turning the world upside down, affecting the nations of the earth
		Movement not centralized to one place, but everywhere, in every nation almost simultaneously

(Regarding future restorations, this is not a prophetic word. This picture of God's Restoration using the Tabernacle of Moses as a Restoration Pattern, simply shows what God restored in the past and presumably what He will restore next, but please do not take this as a "thus says YeHoVaH, Word".) Also keep in mind that in every generation God has a remnant. Those who make up the remnant make well operate as one totally restored in New Testament faith, their life streaming from an overwhelming Presence of God affecting their generation, and hopefully, other generations as well by their legacy.

With buried truth exposed and restored, let's take a few moments and see how those truths became buried in the first place.

AN UPDAED
THE DIGRESSION FROM TRUTH

To understand how the church digressed, or how the truths, so powerfully expressed by the Apostles and by the early church believers, end up buried, we need to take a quick look back at certain events. We know from bible history that while the church spread its arms open to the Jew to receive Yeshua, the eventual outcome of that evangelism, by the end of the first century, on the surface, *it seemed* that the number of Gentile converts, by far, outweighed the number of Jewish converts to Christianity. However, in recent years, with the discovery of ancient Hebrew texts, it's believed the Hebraic believers, (Jewish converts), went underground.

In the time directly after the original apostles died, the leadership of the church encountered widespread persecution of anything Hebraic, and so we find by the time we arrive at the 325 AC[39]E, Constantine enters the scene. Due to his self- appointment to church headship and his desire to extinguish, by force anything remaining of the Hebraic practices, such as Shabbat or Passover, *the church lost its Hebraic roots.* Practising such meant death.

---

[39] After Common Era

Emperor Constantine, in his attempt to remove anything Jewish, changed the days of the week from the biblical mindset of 1st day, etc. to an Hellenistic naming of the days of the weeks after the gods of Greece, using titles, such as Sun-day after the 'sun god' and Saturday after the god Saturn, etc. In addition, he changed the day of rest from Shabbat (7th day of the week) to Sunday, and if that were not enough, he changed the Passover to Easter, introducing practices based on Mythological teachings of ancient Babylonian gods.

To sum it up, he removed anything Hebraic (Jewish) and implemented Hellenistic viewpoints, no matter how ungodly their source, into every aspect of the church. Thus, Constantine's contribution to Christianity was none other than an introduction to a religion, with a form of WORKS or "LAWS", based on practices which made the worshipper dependent upon church leadership and the articles of 'faith' that Constantine commanded that all Christians exercise.

Eventually, the beauty of the Faith and the principles of the New Covenant became buried beneath a barrage of practices, some of which meant believers must gain their own righteousness and earn their entrance into heaven. The practices set in place by church leaders, such as Constantine, and those that followed him, became law and believers no longer understood the New Covenant ways of faith. Without the Hebraic and

Apostolic writings of the bible available to the masses, biblical ignorance prevailed. Also, again from recent Hebraic writings, we discover the Jewish or Hebraic style church, went underground to survive.

In summary, a quick look back at what we call church history shows a church entity, which embraced idolatry under Constantine, and steeped in unbiblical practices, substituted the 'truth' for a lie. Let's call Constantine, a version of Jeroboam. Introducing idolatry into Northern Israel, is that not exactly what Jeroboam[40] did?

Remember, he took the base foundation of the faith, inaugurated by God and practiced at that time in Judah, and altered that base, introducing golden calf worship to the people of his kingdom, and he made practices similar to, or parallel to, God's original mandates for Israel.

MIRROR IMAGE OF JEROBOAM

A detailed study of Jeroboam and Northern Israel, compared to Constantine and his ungodly additions to the Church, have an uncanny parallel. Unfortunately, this idolatry ruined the nation of Northern Israel since she never forsook the religion Jeroboam introduced,

---

[40] Jeroboam, the 1st King of Northern Israel, was discussed in the earlier chapters of this book.

but *fortunately*, for New Covenant believers, that is where the parallel ends.

CRACKING THE ERRONEOUS SYSTEM
God used certain Reformers to expose the deceptions within Constantine's erroneous system. With each Reformation, or move of God, as shown in the previous chart, Messiah's church recovered, ever so slowly, from Constantine's blow. Reformers, such as John Hus, Martin Luther and others exposed to the church of their day the many practices that did not agree with the teachings in the Word of God. Unfortunately, the erroneous system fought back and so, the earlier leaders, such as John Hus, lost his life for his exposure of the truth, as he called the Church back into alignment with the Bible. Still, other Reformers came, exposing more and more precious hidden truths of the church, longing for a revelation to willing believers to embrace the needed reformation.

IS THIS REVIVAL?
As we look back at the church history and its restoration, is it right to call this Revival, or should we term this, Reformation? To answer that question, let us refer once more to the Hebrew word Hebrew word היה (khaw-yaw) Strong's # 2421, revive.

Remember, we concluded, "Revival walls out death or whatever takes away life". An even closer look at the Hebrew root word, in the ancient pictorial language, shows something else rather remarkable. It shows that Revival walls out any *works not done* by God's breath, or, works not done by His Holy Spirit. Plainly put, *Revival removes "works" not "sourced" in God and then, He implants new life.*

Since the Reformation saw the removal of "works not sourced in God", and saw an implementation of "New Life", we could conclude that was Revival, in the Hebraic meaning of the word.

GOD FOR REVIVAL

Today, "Revival", to most believers, suggests an invigorating, new life, coming from the Holy Spirit, giving power to believers to live out their faith, increasing their effectiveness in spreading the gospel message, which results in saved souls filling the churches. Our focus on this *new life*, however, seems *to overlook* the fact that the Holy Spirit walled out, or removed that which was *dead*.

If we are to retain the original Hebraic meaning of Revival, we must consider this aspect. In that way, *we embrace a part of Revival*, which we often overlook, and in doing so, birth a willingness to look at things that God perceives as dead and remain open to changes the Holy Spirit desires to implement.

If we keep that thought in mind, as we notice the absence of the word, Revival, in the New Covenant, we will remain on-track in our understanding of Revival. We will not find ourselves shipwrecked on a false conclusion, over the absence of the Word Revival in the New Covenant.

Considering this, let us redefine Revival and give it an updated meaning.

> *Revival is an activity of the Holy Spirit, Who walls out any works not sourced in God, and then, He infuses new life. That new life empowers believers to live truly, as God designed and made possible at the cross.*

If we embrace this definition, at the same time, we'll see that we cannot expect to see 'Revival' until we cooperate with the Holy Spirit and willingly, without delay, remove ourselves from the practices which He finds offensive, we will eliminate from our lives whatever **He considers sin,** [41] whatever He understands associates with, or produces death.

2 Chronicles 7:14 is often quoted by believers as they look to God for revival. That passage says:

*"If my people, which are called by my name, shall humble themselves, and pray, and seek my face, and **turn <07725>**, from their wicked ways; then will I hear from heaven, and will forgive their sin, and will heal their land."*

---

[41] What God considers sin may differ than what we consider sin.

Concerning Revival, we must *first put away what offends Him, show true repentance*, which manifests in our actions as we turn away from whatever took us away from God. *Then, we can <u>expect</u> new life infused*[42].

> Many believers think that first, Revival comes, and then comes repentance, however, a scriptural research on the topic shows otherwise. First, repentance comes, next, comes a turning away from whatever keeps us from God, and then comes Revival, (new life Infused) after our offensive behaviour in God's eyes, changes.

We know that, since the cross, YeHoVaH will not look away from His people because of their sin; however, He may well retain some things, to release later, in order to help us realize the error of our ways. One thing He might temporarily restrain is what we think *Revival is*, so that, in its absence, we will seek Him further and gain a better understanding of both our part and His part. Thus, we will truly know what to expect.

If we truly want the things of God, truly wish to repent and to change our ways, we will hear His Voice echoing from the scriptures and line up with His requirements, thus correcting our ways. Then, we can

---

[42] Of course, the Holy Spirit gives strength to acknowledge sin, (convict), then strength to turn away, and keep away! John 16:8

expect the entrance of new life, without delay. Yes, when see "Revival", in this light, we take up our part and cooperate with God, and then, we see realized what lay within God's Heart.

As God desires to implement further changes to the Bride of Messiah, to realign her with God's plans, to cut away the blows of Constantine and others, the Bride will completely recover, in every place where the "enemy" sought to destroy her. She will not have the unhappy ending as Northern Israel, who refused to turn around. Rather, it will be as Yeshua promised regarding the church, "The gates of hell will not prevail against her"[43]. In the end, the Bride of Messiah will glow with the Light of her Lord and Saviour, Yeshua Ha' Mashiach.

GOD'S PERFECT PLAN FOR THE CHURCH

Earlier, we looked at a shadow of God's Plan for Restoration found in the Tabernacle of Moses. Here, we will look at another shadow but this time, the shadow shows God's Perfect Plan for New Covenant living.

This 'perfect plan' for New Covenant Revival is found in a passage already well-studied: 2 Chronicles 5:1-7:4 That's right! Solomon's Revival is a picture of God's Perfect Plan for New Covenant Living. Solomon's

---

[43] Matthew 16:18

Revival first speaks of Yeshua, and secondly, the life of a New Covenant believer.

To keep that teaching simple and straightforward, read the following charts. [44] In the first chart entitled "Yeshua in Solomon's Revival", in the left-hand column, you have listed the characteristics of Solomon's Revival studied earlier, which identify the *First Covenant shadow,* and in the right-hand column, you have what *the New Covenant revealed.*

PART 1: YESHUA IN SOLOMON'S REVIVAL	
Solomon's Revival	**New Covenant**
• Feast of Trumpets	• John the Baptist announces Messiah's coming (Repent and be Baptised)
• Day of Atonement	• Yeshua paid the full price of Sin (Calvary)
• Priests Sanctified	• Yeshua makes all believers "priests" & sanctified in Him

---

[44] In the seminar by the same name we will do this teaching in great detail

• Transfers Ark from Tabernacle of David • The Ark rests • The cloud comes and the Glory fills the temple the first time • Solomon's Intercession	• Yeshua enters into the Heavenly Tabernacle • Yeshua's work finished, He places blood on Mercy Seat, Salvation complete • Yeshua breathes His Spirit into the disciples prior to His Ascension • Yeshua enters His High Priest Ministry (Intercession) & believers wait for • Pentecost
• Fire from Heaven falls • Sacrifice Consumed	• The Holy Spirit **comes** (with tongues of fire) • Believers **receive** the Holy Spirit (at Pentecost)

In the 2nd chart, entitled, "The New Covenant in Solomon's Revival", the left-hand column repeats the characteristics of Solomon's Revival, identifying once again, the First Covenant shadow, but this time, in the left-hand column, we see exposed, from that shadow, the life of a New Covenant believer.

PART 2: THE NEW COVENANT IN SOLOMON'S REVIVAL	
• Feast of Trumpets • Day of Atonement • Priests Sanctified • Transfers Ark from Tabernacle of David	• Answer the call to Repent • Receive Salvation by accepting works of • the cross • Sanctified and made priests unto God • Translated from the world into the • Kingdom of God
• The Ark Rests • The cloud comes and fills the temple • • Solomon's Intercession	• Believers enter God's Rest • Believers receive Holy Spirit upon • Salvation • Believers pray for Holy Spirit infilling
• Fire falls from heaven • Sacrifice consumed	• 2nd filling often called "Baptism of Holy Spirit" (receive power from on high) • Life lived out for God, as a Living Sacrifice

Having read these charts, you can see that Solomon's Revival is both a Prophetic Picture of the Coming of Yeshua and additionally, displays prophetically the life of believers in Yeshua. It is a wonderful First Covenant type of a New Covenant reality. It clearly shows how we, as New Covenant believers, must live.

AFTER THE CROSS

As we read the New Covenant, we know that on the cross, Yeshua fulfilled many things. For example, the scriptures declared, in the First Covenant, when speaking of the Messiah as Healer that "by His stripes we are healed".[45] Later, the Apostle Peter refers to that same passage in Isaiah, but in his quote, *he changes the tense of the scripture* to read, "By whose stripes you were healed"[46]. The change of tense reflects the change, took place taken place at the cross, as Yeshua fulfilled that scripture.

Look at the diagram below.

⬅—————— ✝ ——————➡

Healing before the cross   Healing after the cross
Foreshadowed   Revealed
(you are healed)   (you were healed)

---

[45] Isaiah 53:5
[46] 1 Peter 2:24

The "cross" forever altered how God desires believers to perceive healing. Messiah already accomplished it, thus a New Covenant mindset embraces the promise of healing as fulfilled, obtained for us, by Yeshua.

Yeshua's fulfillment of many things at the cross means that New Covenant believers must exchange First Covenant thinking for New Covenant mindsets. Another good example of New/ Renewed Covenant shift in thinking comes as we approach God's Presence. Under the New Covenant, the book of Hebrews tells us that we "enter boldly into the Holy of Holies"[47]

That means, whenever we pray, we do not start, as in the First Covenant, at the outer court and work our way into the Holy of Holies as we pray. Rather, we boldly enter before the throne of Grace, coming directly into the Presence of God. Keeping that thought in mind, we know that God accepts, and pays attention to, us. From the Apostle John's writing, we know too, we shall have whatsoever we ask of Him.

John 14 13 And whatsoever ye shall ask in my name, that will I do, that the Father may be glorified in the Son.

---

[47] Hebrews 4:16

Summarized in a diagram:

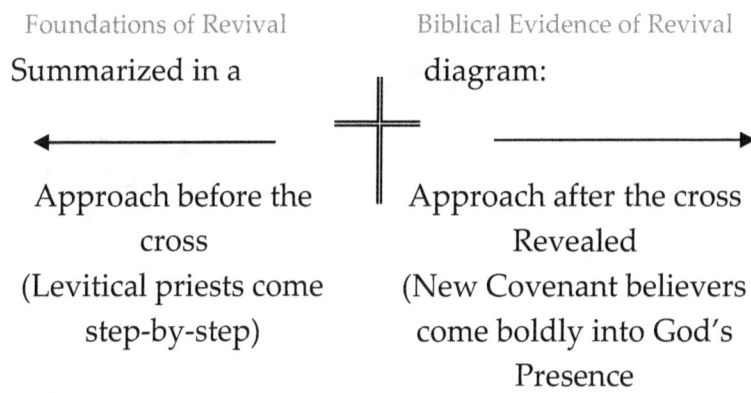

Foundations of Revival	Biblical Evidence of Revival
Approach before the cross (Levitical priests come step-by-step)	Approach after the cross Revealed (New Covenant believers come boldly into God's Presence

Yeshua's shed blood means the New Covenant believer's total access immediately into God's Presence.

REVIVAL AFTER THE CROSS
Knowing that Yeshua fulfilled so much at the cross and that New Covenant believers must learn to think with a New Covenant mindset, we must ask this question:

Did the cross affect Revival?

Considering the fact that YeHoVaH placed the New Covenant picture of Revival clearly within the passages describing Solomon's Revival, we can see a required *alteration in thinking from First Covenant Revival to New Covenant Revival.* That changed mindset reflects *the way* in which we <u>approach</u> Revival. These thoughts are summarized in the following diagram:

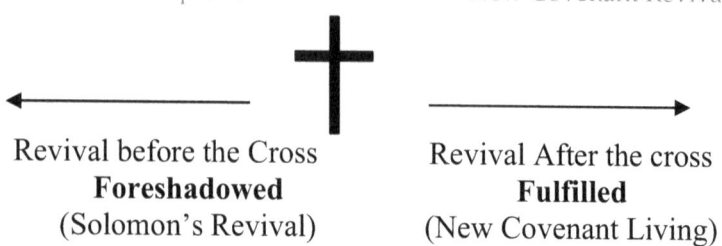

Revival before the Cross
Foreshadowed
(Solomon's Revival)

Revival After the cross
Fulfilled
(New Covenant Living)

Looking at the subject of Revival, then, we know, if the First Covenant pre-shadowed Revival, and the New Covenant brings forth the reality, then we know that God desires "Revival" for the New Covenant church, meaning God desires that the New Covenant church *always live in a state* where His Spirit walls out all things God did not assign.

In God's eyes, then, a revived believer is one who aligns with God's truth, *removing* all things not sourced in God, with God's breath filling them with life. Thus, living 100% sold out for Him, as that "Living Sacrifice" the Apostle Paul spoke of in Romans 12.

Since this is God's viewpoint, we now see why the word "Revival" does not appear within the New Covenant. *Believers have the ability in Messiah, to live 'revived' continually, through the power of the Holy Spirit living within.*

The various aspects of Solomon's revival present a powerful picture of New Covenant life with the Revived Saint, _resting_ in Messiah's finished works, seated within their rightful position, living out their faith in Holy Spirit, Holy Spirit power. This fits in well with the book of Ephesians, specifically Chapter 2.

> Ephesians 2: 1 ¶ And you hath he quickened, who were dead in trespasses and sins; 2 Wherein in time past ye walked according to the course of this world, according to the prince of the power of the air, the spirit that now worketh in the children of disobedience: 3 Among whom also we all had our conversation in times past in the lusts of our flesh, fulfilling the desires of the flesh and of the mind; and were by nature the children of wrath, even as others.
>
> 4 ¶ But God, who is rich in mercy, for his great love wherewith he loved us, 5 Even when we were dead in sins, hath quickened us together with Christ, (by grace ye are saved;) 6 And hath raised us up together, and made us sit together in heavenly places in Christ Jesus: 7 That in the ages to come he might shew the exceeding riches of

his grace in his kindness toward us through Christ Jesus. 8 For by grace are ye saved through faith; and that not of yourselves: it is the gift of God: 9 Not of works, lest any man should boast. 10 For we are his workmanship, created in Christ Jesus unto good works, which God hath before ordained that we should walk in them.

NEW COVENANT PRINCIPLES DIGRESSION

Reflecting upon Church history again, we see that the Church, in slipping into Constantine's error and much error of other teaching, regressed from following New Covenant principles, exchanging those principles for *First Covenant thinking*. This regression from God's established purpose for the New Covenant meant that believers lived far below the destined place of "Victory" Messiah gained for the church, which victory we just read in Ephesians 2.

Digression results, as we saw earlier, came slowly and steadily veering away from the center point of the faith, as believers did not rest in the finished works of the cross, but rather functioned within First Covenant thinking. Many believers do not seem to grasp the principle of rest. For example, today, even while we know we live under Grace, many believers still focus on *their expressed* works to realize approval with God, even after Salvation. Many live their faith without an Apostolic understanding of their position in the heavenlies in Messiah, without New Covenant power and without operating within the principle of rest, in the finished works of the cross.

While the Apostolic writers taught differently, many believers fall into a wrong mindset, living more like First Covenant believers, obeying Rabbinical Law, rather than embracing New Covenant thinking.

NEW COVENANT APPROACH TO REVIVAL

When approaching the topic of Revival, we must approach it with an Hebraic understanding. We must understand what it meant, in God's eyes, under the First Covenant system, and how it applies, in God's eyes, to New Covenant believers. Considering God has already done **_His Part,_** making it possible for New Covenant believers **_to live revived_**, if the believer does not do so, it is clear: *the move toward Revival must **come from the believer**. It's the believer's choice!*

> Many believers conclude, looking back at "Revivals" within the First Covenant, that "Revival" is a sovereign move of God.
>
> An in-depth look at First Covenant Revivals, *part of which you have just done, shows this is just not so.*

Biblical evidence proves that Revival *is the destined, normal state, for everyone who believes in Yeshua.* If New Covenant believers shift from that condition and digress to live apart from its Holy Spirit power, the solution, which calls for Revival, is not so. The New Covenant solution, is to *return to God*, to refocus on, and to obtain what has already been done at the cross.

Another way of looking at it is to first look at God's provision for New Covenant believers, as a constant and steady flow of the Holy Spirit, reaching towards the New Covenant saint, from which, believers veer away.

The solution then, is not to seek God to return the flow of the Holy Spirit, but to accept the fact that believers stepped aside from that flow and must return and accept the provisions of the cross, returning to what God provided through Yeshua. Once a believer begins to think along those lines, they are but a breath away from realizing their goal of renewed life with God.

As you saw earlier in this section, in the chart entitled, "God's Plans of Restoration for the Ekklesia", buried truths came to the forefront with every move of God. What actually happened was this: *YeHoVaH, in His Mercy and Love, called the church near to Himself, to expose forgotten and buried truths*

In their return to Him, God showed them, through His Word and the power of the Holy Spirit, what they earlier could not perceive: buried truths which the Church once knew, truths based on the finished works Yeshua accomplished at the cross God, then 'removing or walling out' whatever was not sourced in Him, breathed in new life, and thus restored believers back to the original foundation of the church.

In other words, God directed seeking believers back to the flow of the Holy Spirit provided by Yeshua, for His Body on earth. Their "return to Him" produced the good fruit of renewed life and vigour in the Holy Spirit.

God's plan for believers today is still the same!

Once again, to summarize the aspect of Revival, outlined in this section, read the chart on the next page.

NEW COVENANT REVIVAL

Foreshadowed in 2 Chronicles 5:1 -7:4 (shown also throughout Apostolic Writings)	• Yeshua's atoning death made it possible for a believer to live in continual state of Revival • Believers live revived, when aligning fully and operating in God's New Covenant, *resting* in the victories of the cross, *seated* in heavenly places in their Saviour, living their life from that place with all things sourced in God and flowing out from God. • God's Breath, therefore, fills believers and thus, totally consumed by God, they live 100% sold out for Him, as that "Living Sacrifice" spoken of by the Apostle Paul of in Romans • 12. • Believers hold to pure doctrines and practices of the faith decreed *only* by God in the New Covenant, outlined in His Word
PLEASE NOTE: When a believer, either as individual or corporately, looks like, acts like, talks like, fulfills God's Will like Yeshua, then present is a powerful expression of New Covenant Life and evidence of a full Revival, or return to God.	

SECTION 3

5
REVIVAL & YOU

Seeing then, that God designed Messiah's Body on earth, the Ekklesia, to live in a revived state, there must be some reasons why believers do not do so. A look at the main foundation on which we stand, compared to what God designed for us, may help us find the answer.

A LOOK AT OUR OWN FOUNDATION

Foundations, as we have already seen, are very important since they undergird and support us. When studying Northern Israel, we noted the foundation, on which they based their faith, was an erroneous system of worship. That system did not give birth to repentance. Instead, it spawned resistant hearts to God's Prophets, His corrective measures, and His call to Revival.

Since repentance and revival link together, Christians must ensure all aspects of their faith, including doctrines and practices, align with the cornerstone, Yeshua, Ha' Mashiach, and following that guideline, align with the teachings of the prophets and apostles. This is what Paul, the Apostle, advised in Ephesians.

> Ephesians 2:19-22 — 19 Now therefore ye are no more strangers and foreigners, but fellowcitizens with the saints, and of the household of God; 20 And are built upon the foundation of the apostles and prophets, Jesus Christ himself being the chief corner stone; 21 In whom all the building fitly framed together groweth unto an holy temple in YeHoVaH: 22 In whom ye also are builded together for an habitation of God through the Spirit.

The reality, as we have seen through our own Christian Church History, is that believers do stray and, in that straying, *exchange relationship for religious practices.* These practices develop into a *system of worship with fabricated additions* that, eventually, cover up the true relationship of what God desires for humankind. The prophet, Isaiah, said it this way:

Isaiah 29: 13   13 Wherefore YeHoVaH said, Forasmuch as this people draw near me with their mouth, and with their lips do honour me, but have removed their heart far from me, and their fear toward me is taught by the precept of men:

Yeshua concurred when He said:

Matthew 15:8   8 This people draweth nigh unto me with their mouth, and honoureth me with their lips; but their heart is far from me.

We know, looking back at church history that Christianity too, has the potential to operate without heart, without true depth founded in God alone. A look at our past reveals religion, instead of relationship, existed and, like in First Covenant times, offered no more than lip service to God.

In fact, even though written long before the church digressed from its original course, Paul's letter to Timothy describes this possible condition well, as he says, "these are people that hold to a form of godliness but deny the power thereof." [48]

---

[48] 2 Timothy 3:5

Unfortunately, just as in past Bible days, practitioners of lip service faith, throughout our own church history, have not always recognized the empty expression of an exterior worship, without heart. Church history is full of believers, on every level, who operated within an established *religious system*, speaking in God's name, yet missing the very heartbeat of that faith, overlooking the pulsing, life-giving flow of the important elements of truth.

Of course, not every believer, in their day, subscribed to such empty practices, without heart. God always has His remnant. In the overall scheme of things, however, eventually, the empty practices produced only frustration, but this helped many to recognize that something was very wrong.

In order to identify and then resolve the problem, God, in His Love for His People, allowed further circumstances to arise, to expose the root of the emptiness or unfulfillment experienced in their faith practices. Believers, with a deeper commitment for the true realities of God, sought His Face for His help to recognize the root problem.

Thus, the emptiness and unfulfillment reached its objective, as it propelled believers to seek God for changes, for what we call Revival, which we saw already, is a full return to God, to do things His Way.

Unfortunately, in days gone by, and sometimes still today, few believers understood that the discontent, and the subsequent failures for inner peace, or for victory in their own life, were signs of God's tearing[49] to bring them to an awareness, of an existing problem. Few recognized that God sends specific arrows of trouble, from His kingdom, with the sole purpose of weakening *the error practised within that religious framework, which fostered lip service and not relationship.*

In our reflection of Church Reformations, we see that few, in the early beginnings, discerned God's action of tearing, and His motive, as to expose of hidden error beneath the surface. Since most people, in earnest, believe they practice truth, without error, they are not prepared to look for something out of order, within what they hold as true. They do not understand, when God sees error, His Heart of Mercy sends circumstances to "tear open" all hidden deception, which keep His people from knowing and serving Him in total truth. He has done this, in days gone by, and He will continue do so today.

---

[49] God's tearing discussed earlier in Section 2.

God's people need only to first recognize the signs of His call to return to Him, as it manifests. To resolve any problems of discontent, dissatisfaction, unrest, or dryness and the like, within their faith expression, it is only a matter of approaching God with an open heart, an open mind and an open bible to discover the root of the problem.

TODAY'S APPLICATION:

First steps are important, and the first step here is to admit there is a "possibility" of error, even in this, our day. After considering that possibility, if we then interpret our longing for revival as a response to a call from God to *return to Him*, we will welcome His removal, in our own life, of anything not done by the Holy Spirit.

We must come to terms with this aspect of God's call for Revival. We must recognize that God desires His People to examine their principles of faith, to which they adhere. All tenets of our faith, to which we ascribe, must fully align with the whole counsel of God. If error exists anywhere, God desires that we discover that error, and remove it.

Leaders, in post-bible moves of God, looked at the practices of their faith operative in their day, learned to measure their understanding of that faith, in the light of the knowledge of the bible available to them, at that time. When they saw the error, they removed it and returned to true biblical standards. These early pioneers of reformation encountered the effects of a difficult paradigm shift, which requires time, and great conviction by the Holy Spirit, *before* the majority of the people accepted it.

Often before acceptance of the new paradigm, the return to scriptural practices hit hard against the practices of others, and this meant persecution, but this cost they paid. Likewise, we must follow their example and be open to God, willing and ready to accept whatever necessary paradigm shifts He instigates, and willingly pay the price to implement these changes.

It is time for us, to be like the Reformers of old, and take out the principles of our faith, one by one, and ***do a faith audit***, aligning all aspects of our faith with the measuring stick of God's Word. It is time we let the dryness, emptiness, restlessness, and faithlessness, operating within the lives of God's people, speak loudly to us, as indicators, to perform a faith audit.

A FAITH AUDIT

To audit our faith means to examine all aspects of our religious life, including church traditions, practised for centuries. In addition, we must examine *modern church* teachings, which may well be based upon Western World thinking, and not on God's Word. We must not presume, by looking at the faith in front of us, that we hold to all truth and do all things correctly, without biblical proof that this is so.

The bottom line is that we must recognize that, whether we like it, drifting faith practices do occur, over time, and thus there exists a need, in every generation, including ours, to inspect our faith concepts, and wherever necessary, realign them with God's Word. Having come to that conclusion, believers, both leaders and non-leaders, come humbly before YeHoVaH to complete their faith audit to learn where error may or may not exist.

While our faith audit, once in progress, steers us towards full restoration, the intensity and depth of that faith audit may go deeper than what we earlier expected, and it may take more time. As we petition God, and wait on Him, He will first ensure our willingness to go the extra mile, to the depths, with Him.

As we complete our faith audit, rather than expect a full answer in a day, or cut short the work of God, we must remember that should God bring restoration too soon, prior to exposing the root, only *surface issues* will experience the tearing and healing process, but the depth of the problem remains intact.

We must be conscious of the fact that when God first disturbs the heart, to stir it towards a faith audit and restoration, He does so to bring a realization of *deeper problems*. Delays, in our search for answers, may be God's reminders that we have yet to recognize the root issues, which show *our deeper need of Him*.

Results of our faith audit bring about one more benefit past that of our immediate need, too. We, like the Reformers of old, find ourselves on a steady course *away from faith practices, which point us to religion*, and find ourselves on a new destination, face to face with one fact, somewhat buried in religious practices: **God is worthy of a people to love Him with all their being, serving Him in total truth.**

When we arrive at that conclusion, our hearts, filled with the knowledge of Him, moves us to serve Him in love. This of course, is the final object of any faith audit, and the first goal to complete fulfillment in God, to love Him with all our heart, mind, soul and strength, and secondly, love our neighbour as ourselves.[50]

Our hearts thus changed, to focus, beyond our needs, to a new target: *God's worthiness*.

> When we recognize **God's Worthiness** for a people who love Him with all their being, we also position ourselves for a release from God's Spirit towards evangelism, which causes us to spread the gospel, not out of a sense of duty, but rather out of our love for God.

Our focus on spreading the gospel stems from that love, and no price to pay is too high, for what can cost more than the price the Lamb of God paid for us?

This conclusion of God's worthiness for such a people could well produce the same words upon our lips as the Moravian Missionaries of old, who sold themselves into slavery for the gospel's sake, declaring, as the slave ship sailed to foreign lands, *"The Lamb is worthy to receive the rewards of His Suffering"*.

---

[50] Matthew 22:36 Master, which is the great commandment in the law? 37 Jesus said unto him, Thou shalt love YeHoVaH thy God with all thy heart, and with all thy soul, and with all thy mind. 38 This is the first and great commandment. 39 And the second is like unto it, Thou shalt love thy neighbour as thyself. 40 On these two commandments hang all the law and the prophets.

In summary, a *proper faith audit* points us, beyond methodical practices of the faith, to a full alignment with the source of our faith, to our God. Here, further dealings with the Holy Spirit strip the outside performance of our faith to an inside triumph, which identifies God's worthiness for a people living correctly in His Eyes.

OBSTACLES TO OUR RETURN TO GOD
Earlier, we discussed some obstacles blocking our return, including such things as erroneous teachings, which assure everything is fine, fostering strong resistant thinking, perhaps even refusing, to consider a faith audit.

Many more obstacles to a return to God still exist, among them, disapproval, by family or peers, whose persecution, by words or deeds, may deter the process. Other believers, or family members, who have yet to understand the call to return, may understand neither the need, nor the determination to remove certain things from your faith life. Keep focused and lift these beloved ones before YeHoVaH in daily prayer, asking God to help them perceive what the Spirit says today, and then hold fast to the course on which you have set your face.

To walk in a full return to God, when others have not yet heard the call, means inward determination to do what is right, what is scriptural, even if others do not yet grasp the truth. Surpass, with God's help, all forms of persecution that comes your way, from well-meaning but misinformed believers. As you do, you will find that any erroneous, current practices of the Christian faith, deeply embedded into the overall operation of the Church, which you discover as error, are far better to discard, than to keep that which offends your God, your closest Friend.

Really, in truth, believers who wish to walk in alignment with God's Word cannot cling to mindsets contrary to the whole counsel of God. To walk in truth, there is **no alternative** but to cut out that which what is contrary to the Word of God.

Every process of restoration by YeHoVaH, in post bible times, encountered *a need to change current mindsets deeply implanted within the very grain and fiber of the operating body, known as the Ekklesia, or "called out ones"*. Each move of God challenged believers, to look past their current belief system of their day, either slightly tinted, or impregnated with error.

Understandably, as believers began their journey to align with truth, most did not know were error existed, nor the depths in which it entrenched their faith. They merely felt faith's frustrations, with an absence of God's Presence in their life, dryness, or emptiness, or any of the many other indicators calling God's People to return to God.

With an inward love for truth, they eventually heard the Holy Spirit's message for change and embraced it. God's revelation of truth helped them to shed error, exchanging it for God's holy and pure truth. It simply took time and a willingness to yield to the voice of the Holy Spirit calling believers back to truth.

MOVING ON

If we are to see a move of God, and soon, believers today must make a decision to be open to hear from the Spirit of God, to know what He says to the church today. When they hear God's call for Revival, they must understand this is, primarily, a call to return to Him, because somewhere along the line, a digression took us off the path of truth. Somewhere, over the generations, truth ended up buried, forgotten, or set aside, and so, the Holy Spirit desires to expose that which covers it up. We must be willing to look for those truths.

Some may say, "Nothing is buried. All has been restored". If that were true, the Church of today would move, in the same power, effectiveness and influence, as the early church operating in the book of Acts. Believers who understand God's Plan of Restoration, even as we saw illustrated within the Tabernacle of Moses, know that God's Restoration process is not yet over, and won't be, until believers function in the same powerful faith expression, as the early day church!

When the Holy Spirit, today, addresses our perceptions of the faith, just as He did to those pioneers in other moves of God, our minds must remain open to receive His Words. *We must not resist any **corrective words or move of the Holy Spirit** as He speaks to the Church to bring us into a full and complete alignment with the truth of the Word of God,* **as God wrote it**.

Once we recognize that the obstacles we face, restricting our walk in power possibly lay within our own *present mindset*, we are well on our way to overcoming them. We are then ready to work with God, to remove any faith practices that will not align with scripture, thus, we forsake them and embrace the truth.

In straightforward terms, we turn our face towards Him and do not look away, no matter what He reveals to us. We "bite the bullet", pay the price necessary for a full realignment, and a return to Him.

Such returning to God involves all our heart, mind, soul and strength, but, with that commitment, we will see the move of God we so longed for, first in our lives and then in the lives of others. Remember Hosea 6:13, to which we constantly referred. If we do our part, we know that He will do His part! In fact, His has already done His Part!

THE BOTTOM LINE
The bottom line of a "**REVIVAL** *AFTER THE CROSS*," is that believer's first understand **God's viewpoint** on revival, and then, embrace it.

As you have read, God's perspective is this: **Yeshua made it possible, for** *all believers in Him,* **to live full of the Holy Spirit and power**

When that expression of the faith is not evident, something is wrong, and so believers must seek His Face for a full return to truth. In seeking God, believers humbly forsake their own ways, ideas and practices and exchange them for God's, in order to follow the pattern within the Word of God, within the context of life in Yeshua.

The fruit of seeking and then obeying God, means a revelation of, or an exposure to, whatever truths lay forgotten, set aside, or buried beneath a barrage of manmade traditions, misunderstandings or perceptions

While the major thrust of any move of God, obviously rests within the power of the Holy Spirit, to see the move's fulfillment to the ends of the earth, *God seeks the cooperation of the individual believer*. If, as believers, we want to see that promised state of fulfillment, we may need to amend our ways, including our thinking! Thus, it is imperative that we take a more serious look at our own part, accessing our responsibilities, as assigned by God and how we line up with His Will.

Once we return to YeHoVaH full-faced, willing to do our part thoroughly, convinced to love God with all their heart, mind, soul and strength, we can then take the next step. The removal, in our own life, of all things offensive to God, will find us realigned with the Word and in doing so, plugged into the Power Source. That re-connection on our part, opens us to a generous pouring out of the Holy Spirit, producing in us, God's very own nature of which we are partakers. The crucified life we live finds its delight in becoming that living sacrifice, consumed by the fire of Holy Spirit; that temple, filled with the glory of God.

CONCLUSION

In looking at the Foundations of Revival within the scriptures, we recognize that God's viewpoint of revival is that, by His Spirit, He walls out or *removes whatever opposes the truth,* whatever works are dead, *whatever stands in the way of life manifested, and we the believer, yield to that work of His Spirit.* Yeshua's atoning death, burial and resurrection provided all that a believer needs to walk with God in that destined, revived state.

God does have a timeline for all things and, as we see, the Church today is close to a full and total restoration, where the Bride of Messiah walks mightily, in Holy Spirit power, operating fully within the Glory of God. Before we reach that stage corporately, however, individuals may reach it, one-on-one with God. God will never turn away any person who seriously seeks His Face, no matter the agenda within His overall plan of restoration.

The passionate seeker, whether in a corporate body or alone, must be willing to shed all mindsets contrary to God's Perception of things, and if they are so willing, they will find God ready to help them press onward and upward, to the high calling that is theirs in Yeshua Ha' Mashiach, their Lord. Any serious believer can live within the realms of the mighty power of God open to the believer in Yeshua, and perhaps, can generate, through prayer and intercession, or take part in, a full-fledged moving of the Spirit within their own nation or other nations in the world.

In summary, then, as you seek God's face, for the destined state of powerfully living, breathing and moving within the Presence of God, you can take a deep breath and know it is not an elusive thing. You can confidently know that God wants you to come, honestly and openly before Him, to ask Him to reveal places where your faith practices may have shifted from scriptural admonitions of the same.

In returning to the whole truth, you agree with that truth, and forsake whatsoever the Holy Spirit shows you, *that He considers error (large or small)*. Then you can fully benefit from His Breath, cooperating with the Holy Spirit, as He removes whatsoever functions in your life that *does not* come from Him[51].

It is more than possible, for any saint in Yeshua, with the help and power of the Holy Spirit, to live within the parameters of the New Covenant, just as the early church. God set believers up for success, not failure, but that road to success depends upon *our openness to receive from God*.

---

[51] Remember the Hebrew Word picture for revival!

PRAYING FOR REVIVAL

Seeing then that God designed Messiah's Body, the Ekklesia, to live in a "Revived" state, how do we pray when we think we need Revival? The answer is simple.

1. We thank God that we recognize something is not right, not working as the scriptures indicate
2. We recognize that revelation as a call to *Return to Him*
3. We then seek God, fixing our sights on Him and His Word
4. We do our faith audit seriously, before His Face, using the Word of God, as it is written, as our guide
5. We ask Him to show us by His Holy Spirit
    a. what things we have put before Him Whatever God considers idols)
    b. what teachings or doctrines or manmade attachments, we have embraced, that *God defines as error* (Whatever will not align with His Word)
6. We then repent of these things and with His help turn away from them
7. Thus, with His Help, we implement His corrections in our lives
8. God then restore us, breathing His Spirit's life back into us, wherever we have lost it!

Our realignment with God positions us to live and walk in New Covenant power, as God ordained. From *God's point of view*, we are "Revived". In the meantime, we must make up our minds to pay whatever costs necessary to obtain our goal, and as mentioned earlier, follow closely the advice in Solomon's prayer in 2 Chronicles 7:14

"If my people, which are called by my name, shall humble themselves, and pray, and seek my face, and turn from their wicked ways; then will I hear from heaven, and will forgive their sin, and will heal their land."

This passage, even though given in Hebraic scripture, before the cross, still applies, as it clearly points out our part.
- We 'humble ourselves' and as such, remain open to receive God's Corrections, willing to abandon anything unapproved and unacceptable in His Sight.
- We 'pray' and 'seek His Face.
- We turn from our wicked ways, (whatever ways YeHoVaH shows us that He cannot affirm as His own. We show Him we are serious about our return to Him[52].)

---

[52] In the Hebrew context of the scripture, it is not a onetime humbling, seeking, praying, and turning from wicked ways, but on a continuous basis.

The result is this, that since we are in Yeshua:
- He hears from heaven
- He forgives (already obtained by Yeshua at the cross)
- He heals our land

Yes, in our "returning" we have "healing" for our land! This aligns well with God's Promise we studied earlier in Hosea 6:1-3:

Come, and let us return unto YeHoVaH: for he hath torn, and he will heal us; he hath smitten, and he will bind us up. After two days will he revive us: in the third day he will raise us up, and we shall live in his sight. Then shall we know, [if] we follow on to know YeHoVaH: his going forth is prepared as the morning; and he shall come unto us as the rain, as the latter [and] former rain unto the earth."

HOW FAR DO WE GO?

My dear reader, how far you *go depends upon you. How much of a faith audit are you prepared to do?* Of course, the positive thing of a faith audit is that it also reaffirms our faith, reassures us where we operate biblically and thus gives us confidence to go ahead and pursue God for the next step.

However, as you take your faith audit, you must be prepared to shed every manmade religious tradition, *throwing away forever,* any form or practice of the established Christian faith *that does not align with scripture* and that was *not practiced* in the early church, previous to Constantine's additions.

In the interests of functioning as God made possible for the Body of Messiah, the serious believer must be willing to discard all faith practices that *expresses only outward godliness and as such, produces no inward change. Anyway, these only hold to a form of godliness but deny the power of the faith!*[53]

> Believers, serious about walking in renewed power with God, in a revived state, must come to terms with tweaking, realigning, or even revamping, if necessary, whatever practices of their faith proves erroneous, failing to stand the test of validity against the standard of God's Word.

The determination to complete a full faith audit, dear Reader, may prove costly in time, effort and in resolutions. Presenting our life before God as a candidate for total truth, in every generation, invites an experience at the foot of the cross some might not be prepared to experience. However, embracing the crucified life is part of the life of a believer. Putting to

---

[53] 2 Timothy 3:5

death our own wants and desires and exchanging them for those of our Lord and Saviour, Yeshua Ha' Mashiach, is part of the new life we have in Messiah.

After all, the cross is where our New Covenant life began, and from where it must operate, the place where 'self' continually yields to the voice of God, no matter the cost.

As you close the pages of this book, keep in mind that, as part of the Church of this century, your willingness to yield to God's Call, to understand Revival in accordance with Apostolic Scriptures, *may make the difference in your generation.* If so, then you and every believer, who ensures their life aligns with God's Word, can expect to experience and be an effective part of the most powerful revival ever to manifest upon this earth.

With such in operation, the bride, who makes herself ready, will move with Holy Spirit power, her hand effectively reaching out to the unsaved living in the ripe and ready harvest field. They, then, will experience God and His power like never before. However, such a move depends upon each believer, even upon you dear, reader! Therefore, let each believer today say, "Heavenly Father in Yeshua's name, begin Your work of Restoration in me. Help me to willingly pay the cost. This prayer or others like it, will rejoice the heart of God. Heaven will be a witness to believers saying, YeHoVaH, I responded when I heard You speak of revival. Indeed, His heart will rejoice for the response He received when He said:

"He that hath an ear, let him hear what the Spirit says unto the churches."[54]

---

[54] Yeshua said this to the church seven times in the book of Revelation: 2:7; 2:11; 2:17; 2:29; 3:6; 3:13; 3:22

APPENDIX

YeHoVaH[55]

A Name to Honour

If, today, someone asked you to tell them the name of your earthly father, without hesitation you would declare it. If, for some reason, you did not know the identity of your earthly father, you would say so. You might even give an explanation as to why that might be so. Thus said, if asked to relate the name of your heavenly Father, today, would you do so with ease, or would you draw a blank?

Most of Christendom, today, is totally ignorant as to the name of the Father, as well as the way to pronounce it. As the author of this book, I would like to join the ranks of those who wish to relate that name to the world. When we stand before the Father on the day, we give an account for our deeds in this body, it would be a good thing to know Him, His Name and how it is pronounced!

---

[55] *Based on information given by Michael Rood. Some from his work entitled, The Chronological Bible, and some from his YouTube videos. For more information see page 28 of the Chronological Bible.*

Did you know that the name of the Father appears at least 6,828 times in the Hebrew scriptures? Scribes recorded it with four specific Hebrew letters. They are as follows:

י	Pronounced yode, or yod
ה	Pronounced as hey
ו	Pronounced as vav
ה	Pronounced as hey

For centuries, whenever the Jews come across these 4 letters they simply say, Adonai, or Ha Shem (meaning the name). They refuse to pronounce the name for several reasons, some of which we will look at momentarily. For now, let us look at whether their tradition affected Christianity. That we can easily do by looking at our Bibles to see the 4-letter name of the Father either written or substituted.

A quick look reveals that our KVJ Bibles, as well as many other versions, the 4-letter name presented to readers is a 4-letter English word, "LORD"[56]. Whether intentional or not, Christendom has followed the ancient tradition of the Jews.

---

[56] *In some translations it is GOD.*

AN ANCIENT TRADITION

In early second century times [57] Rabbis hid the pronunciation of the holy name of God. They did this by omitting the vowel pointings, which are necessary to make the name pronounceable. Hence, as they carefully wrote the scriptures, their omittance of the vowel pointings made the name unpronounceable. Historians believe there were two reasons why they did this:

1. According to Josephus, Rome, under the rule of Domitian, 81 to 96 CE, put to death anyone using the name of the Jewish or Christian God.
2. Many believe that the Rabbis borrowed a tradition from pagans, whereby the name of their god was considered too holy to mention, so they called him "Ba-al" meaning Lord. The Jews adopted this practice and most still practice it today, even some Messianic Jews!

TRADITION CONTINUES

Bible translators followed their tradition for many reasons which are not presently known. It is possible, they forgot the pronunciation of the name, but more than likely, those who knew it, hid it.[58]. Whatever the reason, following this tradition caused Christians to continue in this tradition.

---

[57] *Some scholars believe it dated even further back.*
[58] *According to some, the Jews secretly knew the name.*

Does that tradition offend the Heavenly Father?

If indeed its origin was Baal worship, then we can give a resounding Amen to the fact it offends God. In addition, as we look at scripture, we see the Almighty was not pleased with this, for His Heart desires all to enjoy salvation, including the Gentiles. How can that happen if they do not know upon what name they should call? Scripture [59] clearly says in the end times, Gentiles will know His name and call upon it to receive salvation. Obviously, for that to happen, they must know the name of YeHoVaH (יְהֹוָה).

AN HISTORIC DISCOVERY

Today, some Hebrew scholars [60] have searched the world over for Hebrew manuscripts. In doing so, they found many Hebrew documents have the full name with vowels and therefore the pronunciation of the name. These scholars may different slightly in pronunciation, but nevertheless, they are making the name of YeHoVaH known today.

---

[59].Ezekiel 39:7 *"So will I make my holy name known in the midst of my people Israel; and I will not [let them] pollute my holy name any more: and the heathen (Gentiles) shall know that I [am] the LORD, the Holy One in Israel.")*

[60] *Nehemiah Gordon, a Hebrew scholar, according to his testimony, found the name of the Father with all vowel pointings in the Aleppo Codex, and through his efforts and those of others discovered that name with vowels pointings in over 2000 manuscripts.*

OUR SAVIOUR'S NAME HIDDEN IN HIS NAME

In looking at the Hebrew root of the name of the Father, pronounced *Yah-Ho **Vah'***, and looking at another scripture, we see something amazing about our Saviour. In speaking of the Prophet, the one the Father would send and to whom all must listen and obey, YeHoVaH said that His name would be in the name of the Prophet.

Exodus 23:21 "Beware of him, and obey his voice, provoke him not; for he will not pardon your transgressions[61]: *for my name [is] in him."*

Our Saviour's name, as given by the angel was "Yehoshua", which means Salvation.

That name, with its Hebrew letters reads as:

י	**Pronounced yode or yod**
ה	**Pronounced hey**
ו	**Pronounced vav**
ש	Pronounced shin
ע	Pronounced ayin

The name of the Father (יְהֹוָה) is in the name of the Son! The first three letters of YeHoVaH show it! (Yod, Heh, Vav). Is it so amazing that the name of our Father is in the true name of the One YeHoVaH sent to redeem us!

---

[61] *Please keep in mind that Yeshua bore the punishment for your sins. Your sins were not pardoned, they were atoned!*

HONOUR THE FATHER'S NAME

Throughout this book, and all later books, as well as all accompanying audios and PowerPoints, it is the author's intention to widely use, proclaim and continually pronounce the name of the Father, as well as the name of Yeshua. Indeed, this breaks with tradition of many, however, thus far as we have shared the news of the Father's name and use Yeshua's birth name, reception has been excellent.

NAME CHALLENGE

Since, as of this reading, you are no longer ignorant of your heavenly Father's name, we invite you to join the unofficial network of proclaimers of the Father's name and shout it from the house tops. In doing so, you honour the Heavenly Father, our Saviour Yeshua, and the Holy Spirit.

> *Romans 10:12-15*
>
> *"12 For there is no difference between the Jew and the Greek: for the same Lord over all is rich unto all that call upon him. 13 For whosoever shall call upon the name of the Lord shall be saved. 14 How then shall they call on him in whom they have not believed? and how shall they believe in him of whom they have not heard? and how shall they hear without a preacher? 15 And how shall they preach, except they be sent? as it is written, How beautiful are the feet of them that preach the gospel of peace, and bring glad tidings of good things!"*

ABOUT THE KING JAMES VERSION

Scriptures quoted in this book *originate* from the KJV **public domain version** of the Bible, which means, no copyright exists on this version of the scripture. While some find this translation outdated, Jeanne, trained in the KJV still finds this version helpful, and uses it in all her books[62].

In using KJV, however, it is good to remember the following:
- Some words in the KJV have changed meaning over the centuries. To understand such words, look up the root word in its original language. In doing so, the meaning stands out. For example. KJV uses the word "conversation" however, in its original language it means moral character, or behaviour.
- When KJV spoke of humanity, they said, "man". When you read that word, or hear others speak about the scriptures using the term, "man", know it refers to all humankind, not a specific gender.

Due to tradition, the name of the Father, YeHoVaH appears as LORD, or at times as Jehovah. However, in all Jeanne's manuscripts, YeHoVaH's name replaces the term LORD.

---

[62] In later manuscripts, the author updated the more archaic words in the KJV such as wouldest or couldest.

SALVATION'S MESSAGE

Yeshua, when walking on earth, said this:
John 3:14-18

14 And as Moses lifted up the serpent in the wilderness, even so must the Son of man be lifted up: 15 That whosoever believes in him should not perish but have eternal life. 16 For God so loved the world, that he gave his only begotten Son, that whosoever believes in him should not perish, but have everlasting life. 17 For God sent not his Son into the world to condemn the world; but that the world through him might be saved. 18 He that believes on him is not condemned: but he that believes not is condemned already, because he hath not believed in the name of the only begotten Son of God.

During the time of Moses, the children of Israel, in the wilderness, rebelled against God, at which time poisonous serpents infiltrated the camp, killing many of the people. After seeking YeHoVaH for a solution to the problem, Moses followed God's instructions and made a bronze serpent fashioned and erected it on a pole in sight of the people. Whosoever wanted to live, must acknowledge their rebellion against YeHoVaH, and in doing so, look upon the erected pole and bronze serpent, to YeHoVaH, who gave them life in place of death, then they would live.

Yeshua said, just as Moses erected that bronze serpent in the wilderness, He would be lifted up. This referred to the event, in the future, of Yeshua's crucifixion. During the time when the serpent hung on that pole, whosoever wanted to live and not die from the serpent's bite must acknowledge their rebellion, their sin against YeHoVaH.

Likewise, for those who wish to live eternally, they must look upon the cross of the crucified One, to YeHoVaH, who provided life for them. This was an act of love for all humankind, necessary because humankind is born from Adam, and thus is born with an inherent sin.

Secondly, humankind sins. The consequence of sin is death, and eternal death, wherein humankind will spend an eternity in darkness, away from YeHoVaH. Unfortunately, there is nothing humanly possible to reverse those consequences. Even if a person had made a genuine decision never to sin again, and for some reason they succeeded, all their good deeds and good living would not erase the penalty of eternal death.

There is only *one way* for Eternal Life to touch a person's life. That way Yeshua explained to His listeners as *through the cross*.

Salvation comes by understanding these facts:
- Yeshua, being the Son of God and the fulfilment of the scriptures, never sinned.
- YeHoVaH, on behalf of every human being on the earth, chose to make Yeshua become as sin, in His Eyes, so that Yeshua might pay the penalty for sin, for all of humanity.
- Yeshua paid that penalty. He died on the cross and was buried in a tomb.
- Three days later, He rose again, appearing to His disciples, to show them the reality of His resurrection, to show them God vindicated Him and made Him both Lord and Messiah.
- Yeshua could not stay in the tomb, because "death" comes to all who sin, but since Yeshua never sinned, therefore, death could not hold Him in the grave.
- All those who come to Yeshua, to receive Him as their Saviour, receive liberty from sin and from its horrible consequence, eternal death.
- They enter YeHoVaH's Kingdom and receive eternal life, as well as another gift: **The Righteousness of Messiah.** After salvation, when YeHoVaH looks upon a believer in
- Messiah, He sees Yeshua's perfect life and sees a redeemed believer, set aside for YeHoVaH. Since salvation has taken place in the believer, the Holy Spirit dwells within them.
- All it takes to receive salvation from YeHoVaH is receiving His Messiah, fully repenting from

sinning against God[63]. YeHoVaH even gives the believer the faith to receive His gift of Salvation!

The Apostle Paul put it this way:
Ephesians 2:8
"For by grace are ye saved through faith; and that not of yourselves: it is the gift of God"

When you pray the following prayer, realize we present it here to get you started in your walk with YeHoVaH. Living out your salvation depends upon your commitment to follow through *from this point, onward*. From the moment of your commitment and onward, dear one, please seek YeHoVaH for His help in all things, including help to make your life align with truth, and in the end be a praise unto His name, forever!

---

[63] And against man. When a person steals, etc. they sin against both God and man. PLEASE NOTE: all references to "man", either by scripture or the author, refers to all humankind, not a specific gender.

SINNER'S PRAYER
& LIFETIME COMMITMENT

Heavenly, Father:

I acknowledge before You, Lord, that I am a sinner. I understand sin's punishment is a life without You, for all eternity. Thank You for sending Yeshua to the earth, as the Messiah. I understand now that He died in my place, to take my punishment for my sins. I believe You raised Yeshua from the dead, and now that I accepted Him as my personal Saviour, my old life dies, and my new life begins.

I humbly ask You, Lord, to forgive me of my sins, and as of this moment, I receive Yeshua as my Mashiach. I open my heart to receive the works of the cross that You provided for me through Yeshua, and with Your help, I will walk away from my sin, turning my back upon my own will and ways. I will now live my life seeking to obey Your Word and Your will. Help me to live, from this point onward, in a manner pleasing to You.

One more thing:

Remember, this gospel message comes with power. When you hear it, the Kingdom of God draws near to you. When you repent of your sins and receive salvation, the Kingdom of God moves within. You cannot see it, feel it, or tell it from an outward observance. It is accepted, received, and lived out by faith! Seek out other believers in Messiah and may

God bless you richly as you live your live, now, completely for Him!

So now, be sure and tell someone! Remember that a person believes with the heart unto righteousness and confesses with their mouth unto salvation, as spoken about in *Romans 10:10, which says, "For with the heart man believes unto righteousness; and with the mouth confession is made unto salvation".*

SCRIPTURE INDEX

1

1 Chronicles 29:11 -- 56
1 Chronicles 22:9 ----- 91
1 Chronicles 28:2 ----- 86
1 Chronicles 5:7 ------ 92
1 King 9:6-9 ----------- 115
1 Kings ---------------- 26
1 Kings 11:26-39 ------ 16
1 Kings 12: --------- 25, 27
1 Kings 12: 26-27 ----- 26
1 Kings 12:1-24 ------- 23
1 Kings 12:26-30 ------ 66
1 Kings 22:26-3 ------- 26
1 Kings 6:1 ------------- 84
1 Kings 6:11-14 ------- 85
1 Kings 6:13 ----------- 93
1 Kings 6:38 ----------- 84
1 Kings 8:47 ----------- 45
1 Kings 8:47-48 ------- 44
1 Kings 9:1 ------------ 115
1 Peter 2:2 ------------- 157
1 Peter 5:1-8 ---------- 127
1 Samuel 17:47 -------- 89

2

2 Chronicles 5: -------- 87
2 Chronicles 5:13-14 - 93
2 Chronicles 5:1-7:4. 153
2 Chronicles 6:1-2 ---- 94
2 Chronicles 7:14 ---- 188
2 Kings 15:29-3 ------- 49
2 Samuel 6:1-9 -------- 99
2 Timothy 3: ---- 171, 190

A

Acts 3:19 -------- 107, 134

D

Deuteronomy 11:1 --- 21
Deuteronomy 6:5 ---- 21

E

Ephesians 2:1-10 ---- 161
Ephesians 2:19-22 --- 170
Exodus 20:2-3 --------- 20
Exodus 23:21 --------- 199
Exodus 29:46 ---------- 55
Ezekiel 14
  6 45
Ezekiel 14:6 ------------ 46
Ezekiel 18:30 ------ 45, 46
Ezekiel 39:7 ----------- 198

G

Genesis 15:7 ----------- 53
Genesis 20:1-7 -------- 38
Genesis 49:25 --------- 55

H

Hebrews --------------- 87
Hebrews 11:6 --------- 96
Hebrews 12:6-7 ------- 75
Hebrews 4:1 ---------- 158
Hebrews 4:1-3 -------- 95
Hebrews 4:5-6 -------- 90
Hosea 2:13-22 --------- 72
Hosea 2:8-9) ----------- 72
Hosea 6:1-2 ------------ 48
Hosea 6:1-3 -------- 15, 30
Hosea 8:4 -------------- 49

I

Isa 51:15 ---------------- 53
Isaiah 29:13 ----------- 171
Isaiah 44:24 ------------ 53
Isaiah 48:17 ------------ 53
Isaiah 53: -------------- 157

J

Jeremiah 23:18 -------- 63
Joshua 24:14 ----------- 55

L

Leviticus -------------- 102
Leviticus 16:29 ------- 102
Leviticus 23:24 ------- 101
Luke 10:27 ------------- 21

M

Malachi 3:7 -------- 46, 47
Malachi 4:5 ----------- 103
Mark 12:30 ------------- 21
Matthew --------------- 21
Matthew 15:8 -------- 171
Matthew 16:1 -------- 153

N

Numbers --------------- 88

P

Psalm ------------------- 40
Psalm 85:1-7 ----------- 39

R

Revelation 19:7 ------ 103
Romans 10:12-15 ---- 200
Romans 12:1 --------- 116
Romans 14: ------------ 42
Romans 14:9 ---------- 41
Romans 7:9 ------------ 41

CHART REFERENCE GUIDE

Comparison Pre-Revival Characteristics # 1..........	106
Comparison Pre-Revival Characteristics # 2..........	108
Continuing in the Holy Place.........................	144
Day of Atonement.................................	103
Downfall of Revival...............................	114
Early Revival Traits...............................	116
Feasts in the 7th month............................	101
Full-Fledged Revival Traits......................	130
God's Plans of Restoration for the Ekklesia...........	142
Moving on to Today..................................	145
Moving into the Holy Place.........................	143
New Covenant Revival (Chapter's end Summary)	166
Preparations before the Ark entered the Temple....	100
Preparation at Temple Completion......................	100
Pre-Revival Characteristics (Tabernacles)..........	103
Pre-Revival Characteristics Recap......................	104
Pre-Revival Characteristics Summarized.............	110
Recap of Jeroboam's Failure.........................	26
Revival's Beginning...............................	97
Revival's Call....................................	42
Revival's Promise.................................	79
Revival Stages....................................	112
The New Covenant in Solomon's Revival............	156
The Specifics of God's Plan.........................	24
The Who, When, Why and How of the Division of Israel.....................................	20
Word Comparisons: Torn & Heal......................	73
Smitten & Bind.......................	77
Yeshua in Solomon's Revival........................	156

INDEX OF HEBREW WORDS FROM HOSEA 6:1-3

Bind.............................	76
Come (vs 1)..................	34
Come (vs 3)..................	35
Follow On.....................	122
Going Forth..................	122
Heal.............................	57
Know............................	121
LORD...........................	51
Rain..............................	124
Raise............................	119
Return..........................	44
Revive (Live)	36
Sight.............................	121
Smitten.........................	77
7Torn.............................	58

OTHER BOOKS BY THIS AUTHOR

An Arsenal of Powerful Prayers [64]
   Scriptural Prayers to Move Mountains

Arising Incense
   A Believer's Priesthood

Above Artificial Intelligence
   Finding God in a World of A.I.

Bible Study Basics
   A Closer Look at God's Word

---

[64] This is a book of written prayers of assorted topics to help believers live a stronger, active faith. No workbook.

Candidate for A Miracle
  Wisdom from the Miracles of Yeshua
Foundations of Revival
  Biblical Evidence for Revival
His Reflection
  What God longs to see in His People
Heaven's Greater Government
  Behind the Scenes of Earth's Events
In The Name of Yehovah We Set Up Our Banners
  Biblical use of Banners
It's All About Heaven
  As Pictured in Scripture
Kingdom Keys for Kingdom Kids
  Walking in Kingdom Power
Molded for the Miraculous
  Why God made You
Our Secure Faith Heritage
  Foundational Truths to an Unshakeable Walk with God
Releasing the Impossible
  The Limitless Power of Intercession
  Volume 1: Intercessions from the Author's Life
  Volume 2: Intercessions from Biblical Characters
  Workbook: Both Volumes compiled in Workbook.
Salvation Depicted in a Meal [65]
  An Hebraic Christian Guide to Passover

---

[65] Haggadah (Guide) for a Christian Passover. No Workbook.

The Jeremiah Generation
  God's Response to Injustice
The Warrior Bride-
  God's Kingdom Advancing through Spiritual Warfare
Thy Kingdom Come
  Entering God's Rest in Prayer
Watching, Waiting, Warning
  Obeying Yeshua's Command to Watch & Pray
When Nations Rumble
  A Study of the Book of Amos
Worship in Spirit and In Truth [66]
  The Tabernacle of David - Past, Present & Future

---

[66] Good sister book to "In the Name of YeHoVaH We Set Up Our Banners".

ABOUT THE AUTHOR

 JEANNE METCALF, an ordained minister, believes the Word of God opens a door to help every believer to know their God. That knowledge, once gleaned and retained, makes strong believers to help them stand in the real world in which we live.

With these convictions in mind, Jeanne, inspired and led by the Holy Spirit, began to write in the 1990's. Soon she developed inductive[67] style Bible Studies and self-published them for her students to use. With her major goal to equip the saints, she soon discovered that her sound teachings, presented with clarity and simplicity, made an impact. As long as her listeners put in their valuable time to study scripture and took Jeanne's advice to call upon the Holy Spirit to help them, and they applied the truths they learned, they became powerful believers, transformed, prepared and ready to stand in their generation.

Today, past students who studied the Bible with Jeanne, as well current new students, testify as to the

---

[67] In the inductive Bible Study method, believers learn first by reading and studying the Word on their own, then they glean from the textbook. This study method often gives a better foundation to a believer's faith than sitting through lectures or speaker related teachings.

validity of Jeanne's writing and teaching gift. They love the clarity and simplicity of the Word as she presents it in a refreshing straightforward format. Thus, they encouraged Jeanne to make her books more widely available. Therefore, as YHVH led, Jeanne began Cegullah Publishing to keep her books available, and then a year later, opened Cegullah Apologetic Academy.

The academy with its present online students, received its early foundations becoming one more avenue to present Bible Study material. Additionally, with accreditation in 2024, its development, will rise to its full potential, as we open our doors to more international students. In the meantime, we continue to reach all who reach out to us who wish to be strong in YeHoVaH and the strength of His might.

A greater availability of Jeanne's works *(as well as other authors which Cegullah Publishing looks forward to publishing in the future)*, opens doors for more people to know their God and do exploits!

> *"But the people that know their God shall be strong and do exploits".*
> Daniel 11:32 b

CONTACT us through cegullahpublishing.ca

www.ingramcontent.com/pod-product-compliance
Lightning Source LLC
Chambersburg PA
CBHW071159160426
43196CB00011B/2129